P9-DEX-781

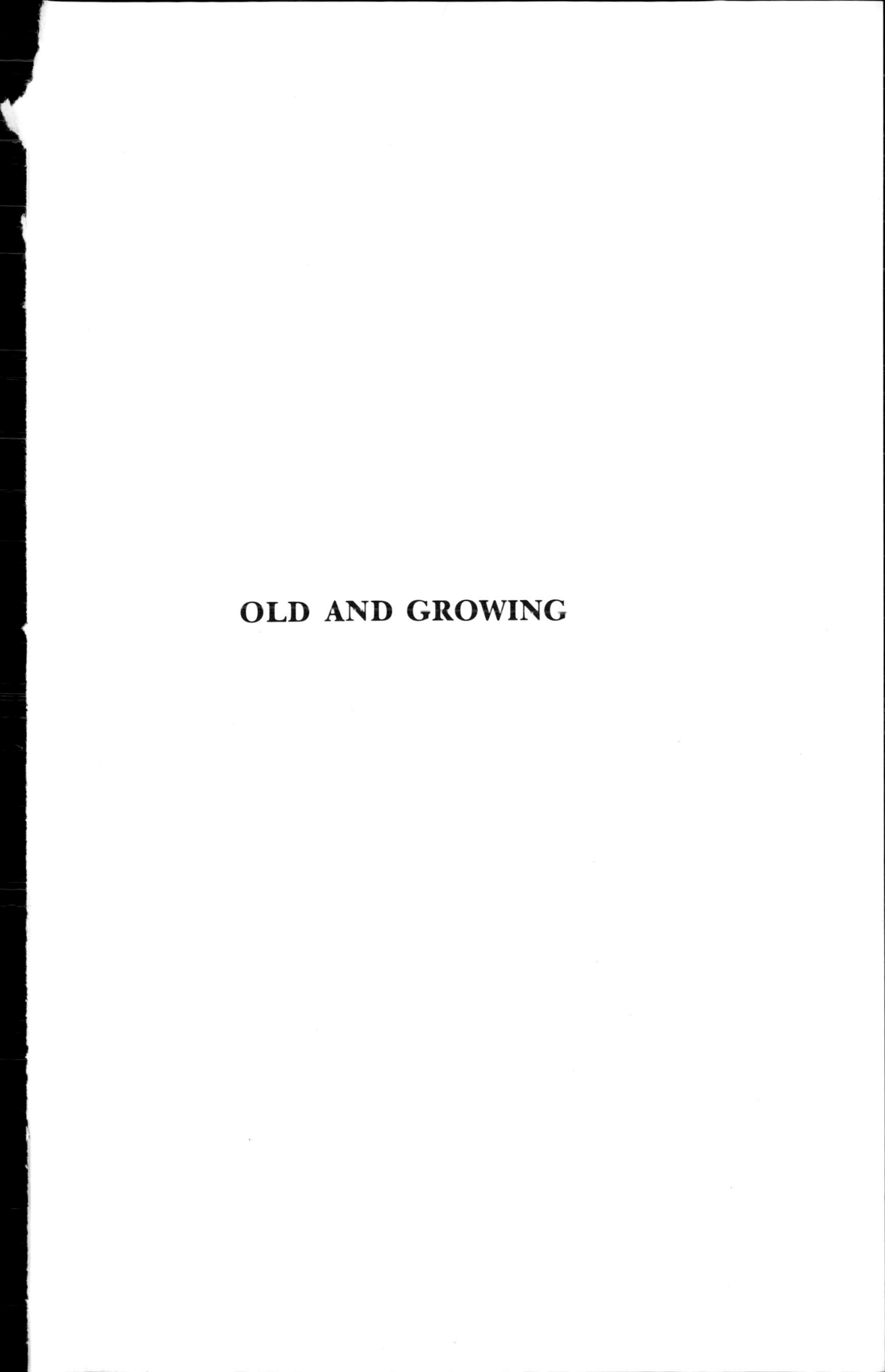

OLD AND GROWING

Figure 1.

OLD AND GROWING

Conversations, Letters, Observations, and Reflections on Growing Old

By

FLORENCE E. VICKERY, A.C.S.W.

Faculty of Emeritus College
College of Marin
Kentfield, California
Consultant to Northern California Learning Consortium
on Curriculum for Older Adults
Founder and Executive Director, Emeritus
San Francisco Senior Center
San Francisco, California

With a Foreword by

Jack Ossofsky

Executive Director
National Council on the Aging
Washington, D. C.

CHARLES C THOMAS • PUBLISHER
Springfield • Illinois • U.S.A.

Published and Distributed Throughout the World by

CHARLES C THOMAS • PUBLISHER
Bannerstone House
301-327 East Lawrence Avenue, Springfield, Illinois, U.S.A.

ISBN 0-398-03804-X

Library of Congress Catalog Card Number: 78-4672

With THOMAS BOOKS *careful attention is given to all details of manufacturing and design. It is the Publisher's desire to present books that are satisfactory as to their physical qualities and artistic possibilities and appropriate for their particular use.* THOMAS BOOKS *will be true to those laws of quality that assure a good name and good will.*

Printed in the United States of America
R-1

Library of Congress Cataloging in Publication Data

Vickery, Florence E.
Old and growing.

Bibliography: p.
Includes index.
1. Aged--United States--Attitudes. 2. Aged--Psychology. I. Title.
HQ1064.U5V49 301.43'5'0973 78-4672
ISBN 0-398-03804-X

To
the "grands" in my life —
John, Steven, Daniel
Jim and Tom
David, Paul, and Kathleen
and all of their generation
whose older adult years lie far ahead
in what we hope may be a bright tomorrow

FOREWORD

As the director of a pension plan some years ago, I interviewed workers who were thinking about retiring and sought to provide them with information and guidance as they weighed their options. I still remember the man who touched his pen to a pension application and then hesitated. "I've looked forward to this all my life," he said, "but now that it's here, I'm not so sure."

In the intervening years, I found that that was not a rare attitude nor one which has diminished among older individuals. Indeed, recent studies undertaken by the National Council on the Aging show that great numbers of Americans view aging with ambivalence and, often, with misconceptions. Retirement is viewed as an end, not an opportunity for new beginnings, and aging as a time of inactivity and inability. But increasing numbers of Americans are finding in their older years that their capacities have not diminished, that their will to do and to be is unrelenting.

That is not to suggest there are no difficulties encountered in the aging process. People grow and suffer and jubilate and change at all of life's stages that flow as a continuum punctuated with ups and downs (sometimes more of one than the other) characteristic of every human life.

Averages of chronic ailments or limitations of mobility and vigor among the "old old" are only averages. Each man and woman is different, and each with adequate motivation can find ways of maximizing his or her potential at every age, enjoying life and giving to it as well as taking from it.

When he was 93, I met Fred Noble. He was then an attorney with a continuing clientele, an active church layman, a widower, and a tender father of adult children. He was also a student at the University of Jacksonville, Florida, majoring in

French! He had chosen that subject, he told me, because in three years he hoped to go to the Sorbonne in Paris to continue his education.

Not everyone can or will want to follow Fred Noble's precise example, but his determination to keep living, working, and learning shows it can be done, and that individual abilities and interests are more important than statistical averages or chronology.

Mr. Noble had a sense of himself and what he wanted to try. He also found the opportunity that enabled him to try it.

It is important for older Americans to recognize their own individuality, their strengths, and their frailties and to understand how much they can contribute, and to make those contributions.

That's where this book comes in.

Florence Vickery was and remains a contributor and a doer. A pioneer when younger, she is now an explorer and a believer in what older people are and can be.

In the late 1940s, when few Americans were aware of the increased older population, Florence Vickery, with a group of concerned volunteers of various ages, organized the first multipurpose senior center under nongovernmental auspices. It was the precursor of more than 5000 such centers to be found across the country thirty years later. The first center sought to provide services to older people who needed them, to offer opportunities for growth, service, and learning, and to enhance self-actualization, in Maslow's terms. She became the center's first director, and in learning what to do and how, she discovered ways of sharing her experiences and insights with the emerging leadership of the center movement.

Some twenty years later, that job done, she retired *to* a new career: teaching, leading discussion groups, speaking and speaking out about growing old in a society of the young.

Some of what she has learned in decades of working with and on behalf of America's aging, and in the process of growing older herself, she shares in the pages that follow. Hers is not a book of lists about what to do or what not to do. It offers few directives, if any. It lays out the possibilities and the options —

with warmth, insight, and optimism.

There is no gilding the golden years here. Always a realist, Ms. Vickery faces up to the realities of the older years as experienced by many. She converses with the reader about widowhood and loneliness, reduced incomes, and the need to find a way to be and to feel useful. But she also talks about the limitless opportunities available to make this part of life a time for new joys, new experiences, new relationships, new contributions, and a new sense of the "real self."

Many years ago, I heard an older woman say, "You can foresee old age, but you can't forefeel it." The author, through her own experiences and through the conversations and letters she shares in the book, helps us "forefeel" old age. She does it with zest. She urges us to take a bite out of the apple of life and encourages us to do so by spicing it with "an ounce of confidence" that men and women can prevail.

This is a book about growing older. No, it is a conversation with a dear friend about growing older, about growing. It will be useful to those who are today older and to those nearing the older years, to their children, their friends, their employers, their advocates. Even that description short-changes the book's value, for as Ms. Vickery deals with relationships, life options, the traumas and tribulations of living — and dying, too — she gives us a treasure trove of information, gentle insights, and subtle guidance, useful throughout all of life.

Faced with a changing world and its new technologies that challenge our present value system, the young as well as the old are often heard to wonder what "it" is all about and whether the race is worth the running.

Florence Vickery leaves no doubt about where she stands on the second part of that question. She says "yes to life in its entirety." And as a reader, I believe you will too.

Jack Ossofsky

PREFACE

THERE is something that I want to explain about this book. It is about aging — a subject that is painful and depressing to many people, maybe to yourself. If so, you may not want to read further, but do not be turned off too quickly. This will not be a naive view of old age through rose-colored glasses; neither will it be a doleful recital of all of the potential losses, problems, and disadvantages. These are well enough known and very real and stressful for many of us. While not ignoring the problems, I think it is time that we concern ourselves with the positive aspects of what can be a most exciting and interesting time of our lives, full of discoveries and new experiences.

Actually, the content of this book is an accumulation of bits and pieces of conversations, letters, observations, and reflections. These I have collected over three decades of working *with* older adults as the executive director of the San Francisco Senior Center, the first community-sponsored senior center in our country; of teaching students preparing for careers in gerontology *about* older adults; and now, and most important of all, of *being* an older adult myself! From all of these experiences there has been distilled what I now believe and want to communicate to you concerning the importance of using these years for increasing self-awareness, growth, and fulfillment. From the vantage point of having celebrated my seventieth birthday, I am convinced that old age does not have to be a downer; it can be one of the most satisfying times of your life.

Today, as I teach my peers in Emeritus College classes, insights and understandings continue to be sharpened as we share with one another our experiences in our strivings to become more completely our *real* selves in these older adult years. We, who are now old, can be pioneers in helping our society rid itself of its myths and stereotypes and develop positive and realistic attitudes about old age. We know, at first hand, how difficult it is to be totally ourselves in a society that is trying to lump us all together and level us down to conform to its ideas of what older people are like and how they ought to behave. Too many people today are still locked into attitudes and prejudices reflecting yesterday's knowledge. What we are now learning about human aging from the research of biologists and behavioral and developmental psychologists needs to be stated in everyday language and made known to all, especially to those of us who are the objects of the research. This is the purpose of my book, as we will learn that aging is not something that suddenly happens and interrupts life but is a part of a total developmental life process.

I have written this book for individuals who, like members of my classes, are eager to make the most of the older years, to know more about psychological needs, gain self-understanding, and learn of the real potentials of this important life stage. The book can be used as a basis for discussion groups for older adults, in community colleges, churches, and senior centers. It will be a helpful text and resource book for students preparing for careers in gerontology and other helping professions and will add important examples to the theories they learn. Finally, this book will enable not yet-old adult children and grandchildren to expand their understanding of, and sensitivity to, their aging family members.

It is to an important reading public that I target my book, in the hope that the older adult years may be, for all in the future, truly years of fulfillment.

Florence E. Vickery

ACKNOWLEDGMENTS

MANY friends, neighbors, and students, as well as casual acquaintances, whose lives have touched mine, have had a part in writing this book. They have shared with me over the years, in letters and conversations, their intimate experiences and feelings about growing old and have given me permission to share these with you. To protect their privacy I have used fictitious names throughout the manuscript. This prevents me from giving personal recognition to each of them, but I would like to express now my deep appreciation to all for their help.

Many others have read portions of the manuscript and have offered ideas, criticisms, and encouragement. They, too, are in these pages and include Eloise Hirt, Maurine Ballard, Clemmie Berry, Ilona Bellach, Margaret Grew, Elliott Joseph, and Lillian and George Pohlmann. I am most grateful for their helpful suggestions which developed clarification and conciseness in the text.

Authors and publishers have been most generous in granting permission to quote published material. Also, I would like to thank the four photographers who allowed me to use their work: Marilyn Burger (Figures 1, 2, 4, and 5), Judy Colby (Figure 3), Karen Preuss (Figures 6 and 9), and Randolf Falk (Figure 7).

Finally, I want to express to Florine G. Miller and Yolanda S. Hurley my very deep appreciation for all their help and their patience and skill in the laborious task of typing and retyping the manuscript.

F.E.V.

CONTENTS

OLD AND GROWING

Chapter 1

THE WINDS OF CHANGE ARE BLOWING

Come, my friends,
T'is not too late to seek a newer world.
TENNYSON

IT all happened the day I received the invitation from the secretary of my college class to our fiftieth reunion. She concluded her letter with this sobering admonition: "Remember! not everyone is privileged to celebrate a 50th Golden Anniversary. You and I are the fortunate ones. It will be great to be back on the campus again, renewing friendships and remembering some of the greatest days of our lives."

I have always known that someday I would be old, someday in an indefinably far off future! That the future had become today and I was now old seemed suddenly to become concretized in those words, "Remember, not everyone is privileged to celebrate a 50th Golden Anniversary." That realization triggered the long introspective letter to my college roommate Beth, who was unable to return to the campus for the event.

Dear Beth,

How we missed you at the reunion. I guess we'll have to forgive you for tripping off to Europe instead, even though it was our fiftieth. There were, of course, fewer of us than at our twenty-fifth. Many familiar faces were missing. Can you guess what words tumbled from everyone's lips after those first perfunctory greetings of 'Hello!, how good it is to see you'? Yes, you're right, those inevitable words, 'How wonderful you look, not a day older!' Humbug, we didn't all look that sharp. Those words, I guess, just reflected everyone's surprise and relief that at least some of us had made it this far! Somehow I always feel depreciated when anyone greets me in such a patronizing way. Such a greeting seems inevitable these days as I meet younger relatives, friends whom I have not seen for years, even former co-workers. Those words seem to reflect the thinking and expectations of so many, that at our *advanced age,* we *should* be falling apart.

When I saw how full of zest so many of our classmates still are and heard them talk about the dividends that life now holds for them, I became more convinced than ever that these years are not necessarily a time of petering out. Honestly, Beth, the reunion was just like viewing a familiar drama, the same cast, the same scene, now in two acts: fifty years ago and today.

You would have loved seeing Fern and Frank H. Frank looked as handsome as ever. Will you ever forget how our giddy hearts always missed a beat or two during the football games as we watched that hulk of a quarterback run for a touchdown? You'll be glad to know that Frank is still running. He said he brought his jogging suit with him. Sure enough early the next morning there he was jogging across the campus! 'It's the only way to keep fit,' he was telling everyone.

Mary Jo Kuhn was very much in evidence, as vivacious and attractive as ever. Since Tim's death, she's back living in her old family home near the campus. She invited us all for tea one afternoon and it seemed like old times. Guess what she is up to these days! She is renting rooms to students! She says some days she thinks she's lost her mind to become so involved, but to live in that big house all alone was proving to be too lonely and expensive. 'There is no chance for me to become an old fuddy-duddy,' she explained. 'I have learned to hang on and hang loose, as the kids say, and believe me they are teaching me a thing or two in my old age!'

Even 'old Lizzy' Hart was back. How cruel we were to dub her that when we first met her as a freshmen. She still seemed as sad and sagging as ever, unmistakably a much older version of her former self. She was old when she was a freshman. Now she seems ancient.

Beth, do you remember how old Professor McCleary used to tell our senior philosophy class that one couldn't say that youth is happier than old age? 'That,' he told us, 'was like saying that the view from the bottom of the mountain is better than from the top. As we ascend, the horizon is pushed back until we finally reach the summit. Then it is as if we had the world at our feet!' I must confess that I am just beginning to understand what he was trying to tell us, so many years ago.

I have rambled on enough, but these long thoughts on growing old seemed to have been inspired by that invitation to our 50th reunion. Do write me as soon as you return. I want to know about your trip and how life really looks to you from this vantage point of being seventy!

Your roommate of yesteryears,
Florence

REFLECTIONS ON

THE IMAGES OF THE OLD IN MODERN AMERICA

Everyone is studying us today. Gerontologists who are taking a hard look at those of us who are now older are finding that, barring illness and accidents, we have capacities to remain vital and active into the eighth and ninth decades. As a group, we are better educated, more financially secure, and in better mental and physical health than our parents were as they grew older. We are more active, travelling to far-off places, enrolling in college and adult education classes, joining senior centers, and, best of all, serving as volunteers and staying involved in community affairs.

I am concerned, though, about the many negative attitudes toward aging that I am aware of today, and I think I am beginning to understand the reasons for these attitudes. Many older people, especially among some ethnic and racial groups and in some rural areas of our country, have been economically deprived most of their lives. The latter years for them are often a time of increasing illness, dependency, despair, and loneliness. Many have become physically and mentally frail and socially inactive because of isolation, poor nutrition, life-long patterns of maladjustment, and apathy. This is changing as programs and services are being developed in communities to meet the health, financial, housing, and social needs of all older Americans. But we are not all ill, lonely, poor, and dependent! The adverse circumstances of some older persons have too long been accepted as the norm for all. A negative image of old age is the result. Young people do not as a group feel close to us, nor do they think of themselves as ever becoming old. They, therefore, feel little responsibility to help solve some of the problems that face us today.

I am convinced that we have a unique opportunity and, I believe, a responsibility to help change those negative attitudes. We will have to fight one of the hardest battles of our lives if we are to continue to be totally ourselves in a society that tries to lump us all together and level us down to conform to its ideas of what older people are like and how they ought to behave.

Further Reflections on

The Status of the Old in Modern America

Suddenly a new dimension has been added to our lives. We are not only individuals, uniquely ourselves; we are also members of a fast-growing, self-conscious subgroup in our society: Older Americans! We, along with other deprived and depreciated people — the poor, the physically handicapped, ethnic and racial minorities, women and atypical sexual groups, are all learning to speak in unified voices. Through such organizations as the Grey Panthers, the Legislative Council for Older Americans, and the American Association of Retired Persons, we, the old, are saying, "Remember, we are here, too, and we expect to continue to be included in the mainstream of the economic, social and political life of our communities."

Although we may no longer, as in former years, be producers of society's essential goods and services or carry the same kind of family roles and responsibilities, we are not willing to be ignored and depreciated in a culture which seems so contemptuous of its aged members and the moral and ethical values which have given our lives integrity and meaning. Understandably, we become defensive when our values are challenged as being old fashioned and no longer relevant to today's needs. We grow resentful when we are treated as *has beens*, respected perhaps but more probably ignored. We often find ourselves in the tenuous position of being physically *in* our society but not really *of* it.

Of one thing we are certain: The culture in which we were educated as children is no more. Change always has and will invade all aspects of our lives. Whether we in our older years remain open and learn to flow with the accelerated tempo of change in life-styles and dress, sexual freedom and marriage, ethical standards and social ideologies, and religious beliefs and practices will be up to the individual. Some of us will be unable to cope with the far-reaching changes that will continue in the years ahead. We may choose to cop out and become reconciled to a limited involvement with life and identification with its current problems. We will become content to be left behind in the back eddies of the stream of history which has been ours but which is now past. For many others of us these years will bring continuing excitement and challenge to maintain our involvement in what is happening around us. We will continue to seek a vital and open engagement with life wherever we touch it.

REFLECTIONS ON

CHANGES THE YEARS HAVE BROUGHT

When I read about the many innovative ideas that are already on the drawing boards of our scientists and social planners I find myself thinking wistfully of the future and wishing I could be around in the twenty-first century to see how it all turns out. Quickly then I begin to reminisce about the days that have been.

Recently a friend and I were recalling some of the crises that have filled our lives. Our country's bicentennial celebration made us think specifically about the international conflicts we have lived through: two world wars, the Korean and Vietnam conflicts, as well as the wanton destruction of life at Auschwitz and Hiroshima. I am constantly reminded of these tragedies as they are being lived out in the lives of individuals who are a part of my life today. I think of the checker at the supermarket with the yellow numeral burned on her arm in a German concentration camp and the frightened, sad-looking Dong family who fled from Saigon during the last days of the siege and who have been "adopted" by our church. I have nightmares when I read about the B-One Bomber and the proliferation of nuclear armaments around the world. I am worried, too, about the slow erosion of our national ideals and institutions and the growing loss of confidence in our elected leaders and government agencies. A kind of public neurosis has gripped our nation, and it becomes exaggerated by the growing credibility gap in foreign policies and the depreciation of our country throughout the world.

The headline in the morning paper, "Unemployment Hits a New High," fills me with panic. The memories of the dark days of the depression of the 1930s again flood my mind as I think about the limited buying power of my fixed income. The increasing numbers of unemployed minority youths and blue-collared and professional workers, the inability of the experts to reverse the inflationary trends in our economy — all these increase my anxiety. Business and industry have become too big, too complex, too costly, and too unconcerned about human beings and their needs. I remember my childhood when the things my family needed were produced in local factories and grown on nearby farms whose owners were our neighbors and friends. How different it is today! Our goods are produced by gigantic industrial, banking, business complexes and corporations with vast power and wealth, concentrated in the hands of huge conglomerates with interlocking boards of directors who remain faceless to most of us. The power struggle between the vast corporations and the labor unions is constantly accelerated, and more and more workers become expendable as megalo machine and giant computers take over their jobs. I feel caught up in the complexity of life which, like a spider web, encircles and entraps me on all sides.

The other day in the midst of the week's laundry my machine broke down. I had bought it only four years ago. When I called the serviceman I was informed that they were no longer making that model and that it would be cheaper and more satisfactory to buy a new one than to try to find the parts to repair the "old" one. Four years is hardly old for an appliance for which I paid a premium price. I sometimes feel that our appliances, clothing, automobiles, and practically everything else that we buy are programmed not to last too long so that we must continue to replace them. What an economy of waste and scrap-heap psychology has been created. Sometimes I have the feeling that many would like to throw us oldsters on the heap, too!

Last week I was heartsick as I drove on a beautiful new highway out to a ranch where I have for many years bought apricots. There was not a tree in sight. Instead, spread out before me was a tremendous subdivision — another example of how super highways are spreading more and more concrete on valuable land that link sprawling megalopolises to suburban areas, many of which are poorly planned by profit-motivated developers. I find myself becoming angry as our physical environment becomes ravaged by the destruction of orchards and farms for housing developments and industrial plants and our air and water polluted by their wastes! Even our natural resources have become seriously threatened by overuse. Chemical pesticides and fertilizers multiply agricultural production but dangerously threaten the ecology of the whole planet. Where will it all end? Profits, speed, expansion, and the ability to think and act quickly are the values of the day. This growing emphasis on material values and a compulsive greed for power and wealth seem so often to completely overshadow the spiritual and human values on which this country was founded and by which our basic humanness is defined.

I recently read *An Inquiry into the Human Prospect* by Robert Heilbroner. He wrote in his opening paragraph,

> There is a question in the air, more sensed than seen . . . a question that I would hesitate to ask aloud did I not believe it existed unvoiced in the minds of man: "Is there hope for man?"

Dr. Heilbroner soberly answers this question with these

comments:

> The outlook for man I believe is painful, difficult and the hope that can be held out for his future prospect seems very slim indeed.*

Dr. Heilbroner may be right, but I hold tenaciously to my ounce of confidence that many of our "people problems" can be solved if we put our present know-how and efforts where they belong, that is, on human beings and opportunities for their fulfillment.

REFLECTIONS ON

THE POSITIVE ASPECTS OF CHANGE

Although I often feel so controlled and manipulated as a human being by all of the technological processes and materialistic values of our culture, I must be honest and acknowledge the countless ways in which my life has been extended and made more interesting and more comfortable by these developments. In my youth there were no frozen foods, prepackaged meats, and TV dinners, nor were there dishwashers, deep-freezers, and microwave ovens; radio, color television, and globe-encircling satellite broadcastings were unheard of, as were long-distance dialing, push-button and video telephone. We did not travel in jumbo jets, nor had man launched space rockets and landed on the moon. We were not troubled about the dubious blessings of pesticides, detergents, and aerosol spray bottles, nor did we know the convenience of polyester, nylons, and permanent press materials. Operative procedures for organ transplants, heart pacers, and replaceable hip joints had not been designed. Lives were not able to be prolonged with antibiotics, chemotherapy, and kidney dialysis. Banking by mail, payroll deductions, and master credit cards were unheard of in our youth. My mother kept the change in a jar in the kitchen cupboard to pay the grocer who delivered her order to the door. She was not tempted to buy things that she

*From Robert Heilbroner, *An Inquiry Into the Human Prospect* (New York, W. W. Norton and Company, 1974).

didn't need with money that she didn't have.

I often remind myself that the scientific know-how that has made all of this possible has been the work and inventive genius of men and women who are my contemporaries. But our technology is moving beyond human scale. The mind cannot grasp it any more! Many of the changes in the way we live and work and move about are too radical and have happened too rapidly! It seems we cannot control and cope with them.

The unrest and violence that permeates our society today is evidence of our dilemma. We know that all is not well when 12 percent of all American families have incomes below poverty levels; when violent crimes on our streets are on the increase; when older people must remain isolated in their homes for fear of being mugged and robbed; where food is being destroyed while people starve; where one in every three marriages ends in divorce; when millions of dollars are expended in housing developments to eliminate slums, only to create new ones; when according to the World Health Organization 75 percent of all cancer in human beings is caused by man-made substances introduced into our environment; when our big cities go bankrupt and must fight for their lives; where the cost of health care has risen 70.5 percent since 1970, and a larger percentage of the national budget is spent on life-destroying activities rather than on life-enhancing ones. No! All is not well in our society today. Solutions for these problems must be high on our agenda as we move into the twenty-first century if our democratic way of life is to continue.

REFLECTIONS ON

THE QUALITY OF HUMAN LIFE — TOUCHSTONE FOR THE FUTURE

When I think of all the life-enhancing developments that technology has made possible, I often ask myself if I am happier and if my life is more meaningful than those of my grandparents who lived in pre-industrial America. I am convinced that in the future the criteria for determining the values of our scientific and industrial developments must be in terms of the impact they make on the quality of human life, individually and in the community. From so many directions I feel "a new wind blowing" across our land today. Through its currents I sense a growing concern about the importance of people, young and old alike, and the need to build the kind of society in which people *really* matter. I take great hope as I become faintly aware of the emerging patterns for this new world and although now old, I want to be a part of it. In the following chapters we will explore how we can all become a part of this changing new world.

Chapter 2

WHO IS OLD? WHAT IS AGING?

We do not count a man's years
Until he has nothing else to count.
RALPH WALDO EMERSON

REFLECTIONS ON

GROWING OLD

"I MAY look different now that I am old, but I don't feel any different. I am really the same person I've always been." I hear myself saying and thinking these words so often. It is as if I needed to affirm it both to myself and others. I study older people on the bus and at the supermarket and judge how they are handling their aging. I imagine that suddenly everyone but me seems to be looking much older. I often find it difficult to acknowledge the passing of time and my own aging within it. I try to hold on to the image I have of myself as still being youthful, vigorous, and full of vitality. My mirror, however, daily brings me face to face with the fact that changes are taking place in my physical body and that I am indeed aging. Then I try quickly to reassure myself that though my hair has turned white and wrinkles line my face, though my body has become stiffer and heavier and my gait has slowed down, I — that is, my *real* self — have not changed. In my youth I thought that when I became old I would be a completely different person. Now I find that I am still the same person I have always been! My self, the center of my consciousness from which I have experienced life and learned to cope with all of its realities, has remained through all the years unalterably the same.

To focus so much concern on physical aging has always seemed totally self-defeating. We can do nothing about reversing the aging process which unfolds decade after decade and inevitably ends in death. But the physical body is not the totality of one's being! It is only that aspect of us that allows us to exist in time and space. The function of the body is to house and be used by the *self* that inhabits it. This *self* has had throughout life its own unique patterns of maturation, development, and growth. This is where we have always made our decisions of how we would react to the outer circumstances of our lives. Now in old age this is where our decisions must continue to be made. From our deepest and truest center we will decide whether we will react to our aging in ways that will increase our fears and despair or in ways that will help us continue to remain interesting human beings with minds that are open and resourceful and spirits that are courageous and undaunted.

REFLECTIONS ON

THE MANY DEFINITIONS OF AGING

Have you ever had anyone challenge you with the query, "How do you define 'old age'?" I have always found that question difficult to answer. I know it isn't the number of birthdays one has had, whether one's face is lined with wrinkles or is smooth and rosy, or even whether one is retired or still on a job. I know now that a concise, comprehensive definition is not possible. The physiologist, biologist, and the psychologist; the artist, novelist, and poet; the demographer, economist, and political scientist — each formulates his own definition. Definitions differ because each is based on different facts.

Chronological definitions are most frequently used by government, business, and industry to determine retirement dates for workers, but these are the least reliable. They are convenient and descriptive, but in the light of the enormous variability in individual experience, they can never be universally applied. In 1900, when life expectancy was only fifty years, it is understandable why a person was considered old if he lived to be sixty-five. Today life expectancy continues to be extended; in fact, the biologists predict that it will reach 100 years by the beginning of the twenty-first century. The sixty-fifth year can, therefore, no longer be accepted as a realistic indices of old age.

The physiologists study aging as an orderly process of physical maturation and change that begins with conception and ends at death. This process, they say, can be accelerated or slowed down, but it cannot be reversed.

Individuals who have experienced serious illness and accidents during earlier life periods appear to age more rapidly. Other factors that accelerate physical changes include poor nutrition, excessive amounts of harmful substances taken into the body (such as tobacco, alcohol, radiation, and other toxic materials), and severe emotional stress and psychological trauma. The aging process can be slowed down by proper diet and adequate rest, appropriate exercise, and positive mental attitudes. Annual multiphasic health examinations, when conditions that may become chronic can be detected and treated, is another positive way to slow down the aging process.

The biologists focus their study on the biochemical changes that take place in the millions of cells which cause them to mature and divide with new cells replacing dying ones. Through this process our bodies are continuously renewed. At some point metabolic changes occur, according to biologists, which reverse the cell's capacity for self-repair and reproduction. Old age, or senescence, then begins. Microbiologist, Doctor Leonard Hayflick of Stanford University, in his studies of the aging process, found that during the average life span cells in the human body divide approximately fifty times and then die. He observed that cells taken from older individuals divided fewer times before they died, and cells frozen after their tenth division proceeded to divide forty more times before dying. A built-in time clock seems to operate.

The research of other biologists indicate that the aging process involves not one but several mechanisms. These biologists theorize that aging is triggered in the thalamus, a small gland located in the brain that relays sensory stimuli to the cerebral cortex. The thalamus, they believe, produces and regulates disease-fighting cells, which are a part of the immunization process of the body. As we age this gland atrophies and the numbers of disease-combating cells are decreased. The body then becomes more vulnerable to disease and is less able to resist and combat it. There are many theories about the onset and dynamics of physical aging that are now being tested in research laboratories around the world. In the near future scientists hope to have the answer to this riddle of why the body ages.

The psychologists' concepts about the aging process are especially helpful in enabling us to understand this period as a part of one's total life span. They view old age as a specific stage in the continuum of life with its own developmental tasks and potentials for growth. I find the ideas of Erik Erikson, the well-known psychoanalyst, most helpful in understanding the wide diversity in the ways individuals react to and cope with change in the various life stages. In his chapter "Eight Ages of Man" in *Childhood and Society,* he states that the self, from infancy, through adolescence, adulthood, and old age develops according to certain patterns and expectations. These demands are made by one's own emotional and instinctual needs and by the expectations of those persons with whom one is involved in close relationships. Erikson believes that the quality of care and love that we received as infants from our mothers, fathers, and other adults determined whether we learned to trust and have confidence in others or to mistrust and fear them. If we were able to trust as infants, we developed, according to Erikson, a positive self-image. If, on the other hand, we grew up not sure of the love of those on whom we were dependent, we developed doubts about ourselves and others that persisted through all subsequent life periods.

According to Erikson, the progress of our lives through these subsequent life periods has been defined by a series of specific events or turning points. The emotional meanings of these turning points have signaled the end of one phase of emotional maturing and the beginning of the next. We can all readily recall our deep feelings towards our own turning points — the first day at school, first sexual experience, first job, marriage, the birth of one's first child, the death of a family member, and, finally, retiring from one's job and when the last child leaves home. New images of ourselves emerged as we repeated or expanded our successes or failures in meeting the demands of previous life-stages and building on these to meet the demands of the next.

The turning points of adolescence and old age, according to Erikson, carry within them unique crises. During the adolescent years the individual must move away from the control and authority of his parents and achieve his own inner authority, identity, and independence. Unless he is able to do this, he remains unable to develop a strong sense of who he is and a confidence in his own self-worth. In the older adult years the self is again confronted with increasing threats to its sense of worth and adequacy. Erikson believes that in old age, as in adolescence, we must again face an identity crisis and find answers to the questions of who we are. Now we must consciously decide whether our inner reactions to outer circumstances will be out of trust in ourselves and our ability to realize our own highest potentials or out of fear and self-doubt.

In old age, outgrown self-images, values, and roles are relinquished, and we must deal with different developmental issues and the stress of new experiences. Psychologists call these situations late-life tasks and include the following (these will be discussed more fully in later chapters):

- Maintaining mutually supportive relations with your spouse, facing his/her inevitable death, then working through the bereavement and aloneness.
- Learning new affectional roles with your now mature children and satisfying relations with your grandchildren.
- Continuing meaningful contacts with siblings and extended family members and being ready if necessary to assume increasing responsibilities for the emotional and perhaps financial support of elderly family members.
- Expanding your ability to invest in new relationships and interests outside of the immediate family.
- Keeping mentally alert and actively involved for as long as

possible in community and social concerns and responsibilities.
- Adjusting living arrangements and standards to the level of your retirement income and changing needs.
- Adapting to the physical changes brought on by the aging process and taking all necessary steps to control and manage these changes.
- Accepting graciously the needed help from caring persons if your own strength and powers fail and dependency increases.
- Growing in the conscious acceptance of death as a part of life and developing the inner resources to deal creatively with it.

Although psychologists, biologists, and physiologists all add important dimensions to our understanding of the aging process, it still cannot be totally defined in terms of psychological stress, biochemical reactions, physical changes, or chronological time. I am persuaded that our personal definitions and those of artists, poets, novelists, and cartoonists with their insight, whimsy, and imagination catch the essence of who we really are. Responses from an assignment to my students to write their definitions of growing old have caught the spirit of how differently people feel about their own aging:

Growing old is when you get out of the shower, and you're glad the mirror is all fogged up.

Growing old is when you no longer have to lie about your age.

Growing old is the time to be truly oneself.

Growing old is learning to paint.

Growing old is the uselessness I feel in being a fountain of wisdom, when no one wants to drink.

Growing old is having time to really listen.

Growing old is when you cheerfully ask someone, "How are you?" and they reply with all their symptoms in detail.

Growing old is doing your own thing and not having to impress anyone.

Growing old is looking back over what I have accomplished

and finding it good.

I have always been inspired by the statement on aging by the Spanish-born American philosopher George Santayana:

> Never, have I enjoyed youth so thoroughly, as I have in old age . . . Nothing is inherently and invincibly young except spirit. And spirit can enter a human being perhaps better in the quiet of old age and dwell there more undisturbed than in the turmoil of adventure. But it must be in solitude. Old places and old persons in their turn, when spirit dwells in them, have an intrinsic vitality of which youth is incapable; precisely the balance and wisdom that comes from long perspectives and broad foundations.*

GROWING OLD: A UNIQUELY INDIVIDUAL EXPERIENCE

The content of our days in old age will have much in common, but the ways in which we react to our common experiences will be different. How it feels to be old will be one's own unique experience. Some of us have felt the void and others an overpowering sense of freedom when our children were raised and established in homes and jobs of their own. We have known how it feels to have jobs that gave our lives meaning and security and then suddenly, because we reached a certain birthday, to be retired. We have felt despair and grief when relatives and close friends have died and the emptiness that then filled our days. Many of us know about bifocals, hearing aids, dentures, and stiff joints. Some of us can still feel the trauma that engulfed us when, failing to pass the driver's test, the car had to be sold.

Many of us have felt an uncontrolled anger rising within us when children, out of their concern, began making decisions for us that were still ours to make. We have gained new perspectives on ourselves through the eyes of our younger grandchildren, as guests who come for dinner on holidays and special occasions. From older grandchildren we have found

*From George Santayana, *Philosophy of Santayana* (New York, Charles Scribner's Sons, 1936).

ourselves accepted either as confidents, who often seemed more understanding and tolerant of them than their parents, or as rigid, meddling relatives always needing to talk about how life was in the "good old days."

As we have grown old in the very neighborhoods where we lived for so long we have often felt as if we were strangers when familiar landmarks were torn down to make room for highrise buildings and parking lots. We have felt devalued when decreased incomes and returns on investments have made it impossible to maintain former memberships in professional, social, labor, church, and lodge organizations and to travel and dine out whenever we wished. Our frustrations have mounted as we became unable to give our children and grandchildren the gifts that our hearts would choose or to support all of the good causes that we believe in. We have often felt strangely disquieted when our churches and favorite charitable organizations seemed to be dominated by new and unfamiliar concerns. We have known either panic or a great sense of relief when we finally decided to give up the old home that suddenly became too large and costly to maintain. Any we have felt the poignant pangs of separation as we gave away dearly loved and highly prized possessions for which there was no room in a smaller living space. Finally, we have felt the overwhelming loss and loneliness on the death of one's husband or wife and the need to face the reality that our lives, too, are drawing to a close.

In all of these ways and many more we know firsthand how it feels to be old. For some of us growing old has been extremely painful; for others it has been easier if we have been able to cope in positive and creative ways so that we have not felt overwhelmed with all the changes.

A letter from my sister this week again made me aware of how differently individuals experience aging. She writes,

> *Dear Florence,*
>
> It's high time that I sent you a note. I have been so busy with a beginner's painting class that the weeks have just flown. You should see some of my masterpieces! They're really not that good, but I had so much fun trying. I've made some good new friends, too. Everyone seemed so alive and

completely turned-on by their new hobby. We all agreed, life offers so much these days. There is never enough time for all our new interests.

I'm sure you remember my friend, Ruth S., who entertained us for lunch when you were here. I dropped in to see her yesterday, and I couldn't help but contrast her attitudes with those of my new friends. She is so negative about everything, herself included. She has almost become a recluse and is so bitter about old age. Amazingly her health is fairly good, she has a very attractive apartment, and is fairly comfortable financially. She certainly didn't spark to all of my rambling on about the things that are exciting me these days or to any of my suggestions of things she might enjoy. It's sad to see anyone let themselves become so isolated and unhappy when life still offers so much. What do you think makes such a difference in people?

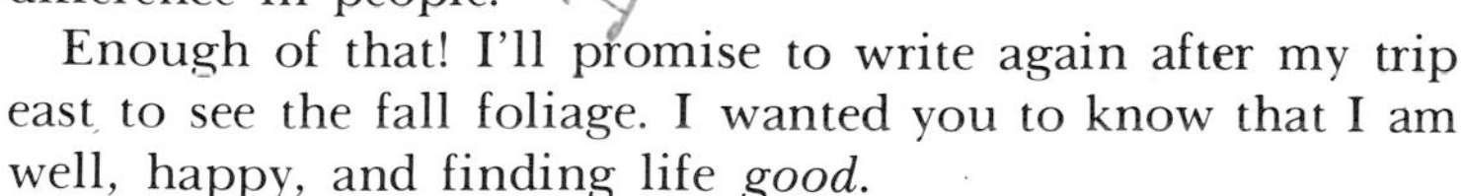

Enough of that! I'll promise to write again after my trip east to see the fall foliage. I wanted you to know that I am well, happy, and finding life *good*.

Ever yours,
Sue

I so admire my neighbor, Elsie J., whose attitude about aging is a winner! The morning that I dropped by to congratulate her on her seventy-seventh birthday, she explained, "I'm trying my darndest to be a nice old lady, to keep my sense of humor and be cooperative. I've known some mighty disagreeable, sour old ladies in my life, and I'm determined not to be one of them. I'm finding it fun to be an old lady! It's wonderful to be able to smile at a man without any second thoughts and pick up a conversation with anyone I want. Too many old folks fuss about the most unimportant things; they lash out at everything. Old age doesn't give us the right to give our candid opinions on any and all subjects. I'll give my opinion when asked, but only then!"

REFLECTIONS ON

OUR CHOICES IN COPING WITH CHANGE

The freedom and the responsibility to decide how we will meet the outer circumstances of our lives will always be ours.

Figure 2. Bird watching — new experiences add zest to our days.

This freedom to decide will remain one of our last sure defenses in maintaining our inner integrity and personal dignity. When loneliness, boredom, dependency, and fear threaten to engulf us, making the choice for self-realization will not be easy. It will take courage and faith and many failures and new beginnings to let our lives flow from our inner centers of integrity and strength rather than from our mounting fears and anxieties.

Self-recrimination for what might have been or what we should have done and feelings of martyrdom and self-pity will be totally self-defeating. We will need to accept ourselves and all we have become with all the emotional honesty and trust we can muster. We need no longer impress or compete with others. We are free to be our own real selves. We can speak our minds and raise questions about issues that concern us. We can take risks and become responsible social critics. We will no longer need to wear masks in order to live up to the expectations of other people. We can now risk ourselves in making the goodness of life and love believable to all with whom we are in contact. Hopefully, we will be able to maintain a zest for living and a sense of humor that will help us keep the frustrations and anxieties that crowd in on our lives in proper perspective.

For those of us who have carried through all of our lives an accumulation of negative feelings and deep hurts due to real or imaginary rejection, the choice for self-realization will not be easy. If we have decided that it is natural for us to be unhappy and fearful, timid and withdrawn, and that life no longer can have meaning and satisfaction for us, we will need to gather all of the determination we can to break out of such self-limiting attitudes. We will need to realize that we can no longer blame others but must accept as ours the responsibility for what we have become. To respond to the crises of the later years in despair and fear will result only in our becoming egocentric, unhappy, demanding, and manipulating individuals overly absorbed in ourselves, our bodily processes, and psychosomatic illnesses.

Who is Old and What is Aging?

Again we ask ourselves the question, "Who is old and what is aging?" As I think about the many individuals I have known who have moved into this phase of their lives, I am convinced that one is old when he no longer believes in himself and fails to continue to grow and realize his own highest potentials. The gerontologists and scientists will extend their research, and their studies will accumulate more and more data to describe the process. Aging, however, can be defined only from within by those of us who are involved in it.

Chapter 3

LATE-LIFE EVENTS BRING NEW LIFE TASKS

> Experience is not what happens to a man —
> It is what a man does with what happens to him.*
>
> ALDOUS HUXLEY

"TENSIONS! Big Trouble in the 70s!" This newspaper headline caught my attention recently. Some young reporter, I concluded, had just discovered aging and the fact that stresses pile up in the later years and bring *big trouble* to many people. But I was mistaken. He was not writing about the tensions in the lives of seventy-year-old men and women but about those created by the many perplexing social problems in the 1970s. Every decade, according to the writer, has some figure, object, or idea that seems to capture in one frozen image much of what life was like then. In the 1920s it was the flapper; in the Depression of the 1930s, the gaunt faces of men selling apples on street corners; and in the 1960s, the clenched fists of social protestors. Now, in the 1970s, the columnist believes, it is a feeling rather than a figure that characterizes our decade. It is the terrible feeling of tension around the recession in our economy, increasing unemployment, and continuing inflation in the costs of food, medical care, and other essentials. Added to these are the energy crisis, the growing debate over the safety of atomic energy, violence on our city streets, and the rape and pollution of our physical environment. These problems, for which there seem to be no immediate solutions, become a foreboding backdrop against which we must daily cope with the normal tensions that are a part of just being alive. Although serious stresses and tensions occurred in all the earlier stages of our lives, in old age

*From Aldous Huxley, *The Perennial Philosopher* (New York, Harper and Row Publishers, 1945).

they become accumulative and interlocking and are experienced with increasing frequency and certainty. Few of us can tolerate the traumatic losses in old age without some upset of emotional equilibrium.

OBSERVATIONS OF

STRESSFUL EXPERIENCES IN THE LIVES OF MY FRIENDS

Every day I become more aware of the many stressful experiences that many of my friends and neighbors are facing. The recent crisis in Ann's life comes to mind.

Because of a crippling attack of rheumatoid arthritis, Ann's husband, John, had been forced to retire from his job as a salesman for a large insurance company. He was too young to draw his Social Security benefits, and the disability pension he received from his company was not adequate to maintain their home and accustomed life style. Ann had been a teacher before their marriage, so she decided for her mental health and to supplement their income that she would return to teaching. Furthermore, her ninety-three-year-old mother, who lived in a nearby nursing home, was becoming increasingly dependent on her. Ann's mother needed not only emotional support but also financial assistance to meet the rising cost of her care. Ann and John managed their changed circumstances very well until recently. Soon after school was over for the summer, Ann noticed a lump in her breast. On examination the doctor advised immediate surgery, and she had a radical mastectomy. Her recovery was normal, and the day after she returned home from the hospital a friend took her to see her mother who had become extremely anxious and confused during Ann's enforced absence. Ann continued to visit her mother as frequently as her own limited strength permitted. One day she called the nursing home to tell the nurse that she would not be able to come for a few days. John had died suddenly during the night after a heart attack. "Will you please give my mother a little extra attention and reassurance until I am able to come again?" she asked.

A letter from another friend Jane this week was full of concern for her sister. She wrote,

> Why do such tragic things happen to people whose egos are so fragile and tenuous? I am so worried about my sister Lucy. She has not been feeling well since her husband's death last year. I finally persuaded her to see her doctor for a physical checkup. He advised surgery for a condition that he diagnosed as the cause of her discomfort and weight loss. On the day she was scheduled to enter the hospital she drove to a nearby shopping center to make some last-minute purchases. As she walked from her car, a young man jumped from a doorway where he had been hiding, grabbed her purse, and knocked her to the ground. At the hospital the doctor found that, in addition to severe body bruises, her arm was broken. She has had such a difficult time these weeks bathing, dressing, and preparing her meals, I tried to persuade her to come to stay with George and me until her arm mended, but she refused. I've tried to do everything I could to help her, but it has been hard. Her arm, of course, will heal in time, and eventually the surgery that had been scheduled will be performed. What has not healed, and probably never will, is her paralyzing fear and apprehension about living alone and going out even in broad daylight. It is so tragic to see her becoming a virtual prisoner within her own home, and fearful of all strangers who come to her door! I wish I knew how I could help her. Do you have any suggestions? I would surely appreciate them.
>
> *My love to you,*
> *Jane*

Fears about the adequacy of your income and whether you will have enough capital to last and meet the cost of a terminal illness also create serious stress for many of us. This is especially so if you have outlived family members and have no children or nearby relatives able and willing to concern themselves. My uncle Charlie, a widower for twenty years, died not long ago at the age of eighty-six. I had often talked with him about his fears of running out of money. His savings had dwindled during the years, and he had been living a pinchpenny existence. Uncle Charlie still had a $10,000 savings account that he had set up years ago at 3 percent interest which he refused to touch, not even to reinvest at a higher interest rate. "That's to pay for my last illness and funeral," he told me. Uncle Charlie did not recognize that at eighty-five he did not have to save for a long future. He didn't need $10,000 for a last illness. He was ill just three days before he died. Why do so many of us worry about what "might" happen and deny ourselves some of the small pleasures and joys of the present?

My friend Frances was much wiser. She had financial problems, but she was more realistic in the way she met them. I met her in an antique store one day when I dropped in to inquire the price of a beautiful bowl I had seen in the window. She was talking with the shop owner, and laid out on the counter between them was an array of cut glass, hand-painted china, and an assortment of bric-a-brac. I am sure she caught my questioning look and, quite openly and without embarrassment, told me of the decisions she had recently made.

Too much of her capital, she told me, was locked into her house, and it was taking too much income to support it, and too little was left to support herself. "I have decided to sell and move to that new apartment building where several of my friends live," she confided. "Since the children aren't interested in this stuff, I'm saving a few of the pieces that I really prize and am selling the rest." Then she told me about the recent visit from her children and how they had chosen things they admired and could use and encouraged her to sell the rest. " 'Don't save the old house and those family heirlooms for us, Mom,' they told me. 'We like modern stuff.' It really made me feel good when they assured me that with their education and start in life they now felt responsible for themselves and their own families. 'It will take a load off of us just to know that you are happy and have friends and enough income to do some of the things you enjoy,' they assured me." Then, almost as if talking to herself, she said, "Don't I have the greatest children?" I could certainly agree that she does!

I received some tips on how to manage my money and minimize the stress around financial matters in talking with my friend Mary Rogers, who has just published a book, *Women and Money*. She advises older adults to

- Share with your spouse all information about income, investments, and insurances and the whereabouts of all important papers. This information should be recorded in a ledger, and each should know where it is kept. If you live alone, some family member or close friend should know where your personal record ledger is kept.
- Make a will. Without it you are failing to insure that your estate will be distributed the way you want it to be. Keep a copy of your will with your personal record ledger and include in the back the names of your lawyer, doctor, clergyman, and your burial arrangements.
- Make an operating budget based on your income and regular monthly expenditures. Then you will know what leeway you have and what you can spend.
- Why develop a false feeling of poverty and think you can't afford something when you really can? Send to the Superintendent of Documents, U. S. Government Printing Office, Washington, D. C. 20492, for the following pamphlets:
  "A Guide to Budgeting for the Retired Couple."
  "Tax Benefits for Older Americans."
- Sell life insurance purchased early in life to provide an "instant estate" for your children. Reinvest this money at higher interest for your current use. Live now and do not try to save money for the next generation.
- Do not own stocks that go up and down if you are unable to handle uncertainty and stress.
- Do not invest precious capital in your own small post-retirement business if you are not temperamentally able to take risks and lose money.
- Do not for sentimental reasons hold on to stocks or investments you have inherited if you can get a larger return on your money from another source.
- Do not lend money to your children that you cannot afford to give them. You can thus avoid misunderstandings and heartaches. It is better for them to borrow through regular lending channels.
- Have someone in whom you have confidence act as your

advocate. They can ask questions for clarification when you consult your lawyer, banker, or doctor.

SOME OBSERVATIONS ON

THE EFFECTS OF STRESS

I have thought a great deal about stress and its effect on the body and the mind as I have recalled the experiences of my friends, Ann, Lucy, Fran, and Uncle Charlie. I recognize that no one, either young or old, can escape stressful experiences, and that we all differ in how much stress we can tolerate without breaking emotionally. What may be stressful to me may not bother you. You might see a situation as a challenge, and I might feel trapped by it. On the other hand, what looks to you like a real problem may seem like a breeze to me. Some of us have always been able to handle problems and maintain an optimistic outlook on life. Others have been worried and apprehensive about what *might* happen. I have known many older adults who seemed to become immobilized by the crises in old age and have been unable to take any positive steps to solve their problems.

In order to learn more about stress and its effect on our lives, I read *Stress Without Distress* by Doctor Hans Seyle, a recognized authority on the subject. He defines stress as the body's physical, emotional, and chemical reactions to experiences that frighten, confuse, and endanger it. To handle such psychological stresses, our bodies, according to Doctor Seyle, provide a corrective in hormones that are released from adrenal and pituitary glands. These speed through the system, causing the heart to beat faster and the blood vessels to contract, thus forcing the blood to flow more rapidly through the entire body. It is thus energized and enabled to meet and cope with threatening situations.

We all react differently to stress. Some of us suffer intestinal upsets or headaches. Others of us lose our appetites or experience indigestion and diarrhea. Still others may experience quickening heart beats and sleeplessness. The body becomes highly susceptible to attacks in its weakest areas if these stresses become more severe than the body can adjust to. Prolonged tensions, according to Doctor Seyle, often lead to heart attacks, strokes, and ulcers. Studies show that approximately 70 percent of all individuals who seek medical attention are suffering from ailments brought about not by germs but by prolonged emotional stress. Such stress responses can be greatly reduced if one can learn to let go and relax those parts of the body that are affected. The blood is then allowed to flow without restrictions. Many new techniques are being developed today to teach us relaxation including controlling the body's automatic responses through biofeedback, massage, autogenic and yoga exercises, deep breathing, and meditation (we will discuss these more fully in a later chapter). These, along with walking, swimming, jogging, and dancing, are all recommended to help us relax.

SOME OBSERVATIONS OF

THE PSYCHOLOGICAL STRATEGIES WE USE TO COPE WITH STRESS

We have used all through our lives many psychological strategies that help us maintain our sense of well-being and control when we were faced with fears, frustration, and anxieties. Psychologists call these strategies defense mechanisms. They temporarily helped us through stressful situations until we could regain our emotional balance and strength to face the reality. In the older adult years we continue to depend on these defense mechanisms.

• Alice T., a member of one of my classes, was able to handle a very painful situation by making up an explanation that helped her hide her true feelings and save face with her classmates. For weeks she had talked about her plans to go to New York to spend Christmas with her son and his family whom she had not seen for three years. Descriptions of the gifts that she was making to take to her grandchildren and the clothes that she had bought for the trip were all eagerly shared with her friends. The week before she was to leave, it was apparent that all was not well with Alice. There was no bounce in her spirit or spring in her step. As questions were asked Alice explained with a forced smile and in an almost flippant manner, "I had a wonderful letter from my son telling me about the exciting invitation that he and his wife and children have had to join friends over Christmas for a ski holiday in Colorado. He said that he hoped I wouldn't be too disappointed to have my plans cancelled and that he would plan for me to come for a visit sometime later." Alice bravely commented, "It's just as well they can't have me. My arthritis has been so bad lately that I'll be much more comfortable staying home and sleeping in my own bed."

• I know many residents of Springwood, a retirement home, where I often visit a good friend. Recently in the hall I met a new resident and stopped to greet her. In response to my "good morning," she replied, "There's nothing good about this morning!" Then from her mouth flowed an almost incoherent stream of angry words. "My children really kidnapped me," explained Mrs. B. "They forced me to sell my home, leave all my friends, and come to live here. I just hate this place!"

As she calmed down we went to a nearby lounge where we could talk, and I soon learned her story. She had been a widow for six years. After her husband's death she had remained living in her home in a small midwestern community where she had raised her two sons and where all of her friends lived. Last winter she had contracted a severe illness, and each of her sons had made several trips back to their hometown to see her and make plans for her care after she was released from the hospital. They found an excellent companion to live with her, and all had gone well until the companion herself became ill and had to give up the job. Mrs. S.'s voice again became loud and angry. "Do you know what happened?" Since neither of my sons could leave his job again, one of my daughters-in-law came to help me sell my home, pack my things, and move to California. She told me my sons had decided that they just couldn't have me living so far away when I was not well. So here I am. They just kidnapped me, and I don't like this place one bit!"

Soon Mrs. S. was comfortably, but far from happily, settled in her apartment in Springwood. The administrator told me that telephone calls come frequently from her sons or their wives, but they come to see her only occasionally. Although she is very bitter and feels that she has been neglected and forgotten by her family, she always explains to other residents, "I have two such wonderful sons. They are both very successful and important businessmen, so I can't expect them to take time from their busy lives to visit me."

The ability of Alice and Mrs. S. to rationalize and make up for themselves acceptable reasons for their children's seeming neglect and thoughtlessness helped them to handle temporarily their deep hurts and despair.

• My neighbor Elaine and I often drop in on one another for a morning chat and a second cup of coffee. One morning when I stopped by, Elaine seemed quieter than usual and a bit pale. Worried, I asked her if everything was all right. "Oh, yes," she replied, "I just don't seem to have much pep today. I didn't sleep at all well last night, but there's no reason to worry about a little thing like that. I'll feel better tomorrow."

But Elaine didn't feel better the next day or the day after that or for a succession of days. Her daughter finally insisted that she see her doctor. "A slight heart attack" was his diagnosis.

Elaine had felt so anxious over the possibility that there might be something seriously wrong with her that she had tried to deny her apprehensions, hoping that her tiredness and pain would go away. At first I took Elaine's efforts to minimize her feelings of distress as courage, but I soon recognized it as a denial strategy, for I have used it often myself. When I have wanted to turn away from a hard reality, I have tried not to think about it and forced myself to be falsely cheerful. I have learned, however, that a stressful situation can be denied for only a short time. Eventually it must be faced.

• Mr. T. is a patient in a nursing home where I often visit. I have watched how he handles his increasing fears and frustrations as his helplessness and dependency increase. If his bath is late, his coffee is not as hot as he likes, or his newspaper has been put on the wrong side of his table, he goes into a temper tantrum, whining and calling impatiently for someone to come and help him. When he is successful in capturing someone's attention, he invokes help with pleas of misery and cries of self-pity. Through such regressive and manipulative behavior, he tries to elicit the sympathy and support of those whom he believes are stronger and who will protect and care for him as his self-mastery and control are lost.

• Sometimes the frustrations in our later years become so overwhelming that we feel totally inadequate to cope with them. We capitulate to these fears and anxieties and revert to fantasies and dreams of being a child again, fed, nurtured, and cared for by our parents. Elizabeth C., one of my students, is an eighty-year-old woman with great awareness and deep understanding of psychological insights and human behavior. She has a practice, when troubled, of writing in her "soul-cleansing" diary. This, she explained, was not a report of happenings, but a kind of automatic writing, just letting the words come out of their own accord, without selecting, without control, without knowledge. She switches off her attention and thinking, judgment becomes nonexistent, and what is in her unconscious becomes recorded. One day she shared with the class this account of her experiences of regression into infantile behavior and longings and the self-clarification that followed. She reported,

> The day began early. I woke up at 5 o'clock in a miserable mood. A review of the situation brought only disgust. My husband is 86 years old, sick, weak, a shadow of his former self. My days go by with the preparation of three meals, with keeping the house in a semblance of order with the help of a mess of "glory holes." Books and papers get lost in disorder. I do not recognize myself anymore. My reading has become superficial. I resent writing. Out of a scholar I have become a grumbling housewife with a chip on my shoulder.
>
> To get hold of my disgust and despair I started one morning to resume writing in my diary. After writing for some time the flow stopped, and I read what had gone down on the paper. Lo and behold, there appeared a strange creature, a cry-baby, an infant who took herself as the center of the universe, who demanded attention and wanted to be

taken care of like royalty, with obedient servants dancing around her.

Looking at this uninvited, undigested outbreak of early childhood emotions, the explanation of my present strange behavior suddenly dawned on me. In my discontent I was not my actual age of 80. My infant days had taken over and created all the puzzling, incomprehensive behavior of the last year, the disorder, the whining, the need to lie down and pass the time in thoughtless dozing, the inability to maintain a continuity of thought, and to keep my home in order.

There it all was clearly written down in the distortion of my free flowing associations. I lived behind a wall of resistance against the actual life around me, afraid of the requirements of the day. When I accused my husband and others of being responsible for my dreary life, I simply staged my own conditions and used my weakness as a screen. I was actually in a state of relapse into my childish ways and did not want to acknowledge my regression into the phase of infantile helplessness. It is easier to find faults in others than in ourselves, but beauty is in the eye of the beholder and so is ugliness and distortion. This insight into the actual state of my emotions had the effect of a shock. Here I was on the way to helpless invalidism and old age senility. The horror of that prospect made the wall of resistance dissolve like fog in the sun. I had been rejecting the insights and the truth about my own weaknesses. Instead of demanding care for myself I saw and felt that I was now able to care for others and myself as well.

By the use of rationalization, denial and manipulation, and regression, all of the individuals presented in this chapter have been able to cope with the reality of their day-by-day problems.

Other defense mechanisms we frequently use include exclusion of unwanted stimuli, whereby we fail to hear or see what is disturbing to us; sublimation, when we find substitute channels through which to express natural instinctive feelings; reminiscing, when we recall and dwell on happier periods of our lives in order to blot out the hurts and disappointments of the present; aggressive behavior, whereby we attempt to compensate for our loss of self-confidence and inner security; and social withdrawal, in which we indulge to protect ourselves from rejection. We all use these strategies which often overlap to help maintain our mental health during our times of crises and stress.

There are some older adults, however, who have been left so drained of all emotional resources by the many stresses they have experienced that even the use of these defense mechanisms are ineffective in preventing them from slipping into deep mental depression and psychosomatic illnesses. Extended periods of depression for such individuals can often be alleviated by short-term counselling help. Others may need more intensive individual or group psychotherapy and even hospitalization. For most of us normal depression can be reduced to manageable levels by experiences that give us continuing emotional supports, such as improvement in strained family relationships, a confidant relationship with another person, and re-involvement of ourselves in stimulating interests and useful activities.

The increased use of drugs and alcohol by older people as a crutch to help forget for a time the many things that disturb them has risen to alarming proportions. It is estimated that over 5 percent of all Americans sixty-five years and older may be classified as chronic alcoholics. Alcohol for many becomes an escape that helps maintain a denial position about realities that have become too uncomfortable to bear.

A shocking number of older adults are also turning to the indiscriminate use of both prescription and nonprescription tranquilizing drugs. These do calm the nerves and may temporarily deaden feelings of distress, but they do not solve the fundamental problems that cause depression. Often doctors who cannot find a physical basis for depression prescribe one of the new chemical mood-elevating drugs, without being aware of any current life circumstances that may have triggered the depression. It is estimated that $200 million are spent annually in this country by all age groups for tranquilizers and sedatives. Since the medical profession still lacks full knowledge of how these drugs work, their uncontrolled use raises many questions. Although tensions and stresses in the older adult years are most difficult to handle, they do play a vital role in maintaining mental health, for they indicate when something is wrong that needs to be changed. When tensions are removed by drugs or alcohol, the problems are never faced and never resolved, only postponed.

When serious depression continues unrelieved, some individuals become so desperate that they give up the struggle and take their own lives. We older adults make up about 10 percent of the population of this country, but we account for 25 percent of all suicides. In addition, instead of actually taking their lives, many severely depressed persons unconsciously will their own deaths by refusing to eat, follow their doctors' orders, or take prescribed medication.

SOME REFLECTIONS ON

MAINTAINING MENTAL HEALTH IN THE OLDER ADULT YEARS

We have since childhood been programmed to hide our true feelings. I was very embarrassed and uncomfortable when I offered my sympathy to a friend who had recently lost her sister. She burst into uncontrollable crying and then apologized profusely for having done so. It has become a mark of emotional maturity in our culture to suppress any expression of our deepest feelings. As a result we hold too tight a rein on them, fearing that we will be judged weak and lacking in self-control. It is acceptable for women to cry when they are upset, but such behavior by men is considered unmanly and weak. Men have to supress and internalize their true feelings. They are expected to be in control in all situations. This may explain why more men than women are victims of heart attacks and other degenerative diseases and die earlier than women.

All through our lives we have experienced periods when we felt depressed and blue. These may occur with greater frequency and intensity as we grow older because of the increasing losses that we will experience and our unresolved grief, guilt, and loneliness. Some of us will find help in working for a short time with a psychotherapist. Many older adults are finding supportive and understanding help through a program found in many communities called Rehabilitation Counselling. This program is based on a theory developed by Harvey Jackens who believes that it is necessary to "discharge" our emotions and tensions in order to be rid of them. This can be done best by talking with another individual who becomes your co-counsellor, who makes himself or herself available whenever you feel distressed and need help. The co-counsellor listens while the counselee talks out his feelings. The co-counsellor makes no comments or suggestions; he only gives his quiet attention and support. Then the roles are switched, and the co-counsellor now becomes the one who has an opportunity to discharge, in any way that is helpful, the feelings about things that are bugging him. We all need such a network of understanding friends to whom we can express our true feelings without being apologetic or defensive. Over-protection and efforts to infantilize us by well-meaning children and relatives will be of little help.

Even though we may be fortunate enough to be surrounded by a multitude of concerned children and friends, they are powerless to give us those things that we now long for: the return of our youth and vigor, health, and personal attractiveness, the happiness that we experienced in the earlier periods of our lives, and the loved persons whom we have lost. Those who love us can give their understanding and support, but these will not be enough if our needs have become insatiable because we have not learned to cope with our own losses and to love and feel good about ourselves.

Chapter 4

THE NEED FOR LOVE CANNOT BE RETIRED

As fair art thou, my bonnie lass,
So deep in luve am I:
And I will luve thee still, my dear,
Till a' the seas gang dry:

Till a' the seas gang dry, my dear,
And the rocks melt wi' the sun;
I will luve thee still, my dear,
While the sands o' life shall run.

ROBERT BURNS

REFLECTIONS ON

THE MARRIAGE RELATIONSHIP IN THE LATER YEARS

FOR most of us the many years since we promised "to love and cherish until death do us part" have not been all joy and bliss. They have been punctuated, at times, by severe personal and family crises that are inherent in all marriages and family living. There have been periods of deep down happiness and a pervading sense of well-being along with periods of doubt and uncertainty: the achievement of shared intimacy and sexual compatibility; the birth of children and the deaths of older family members; the security and insecurity of jobs; the long periods of just "marking time," waiting endlessly for something to happen; the successes and failures in attaining life goals — in each of these experiences we have felt either satisfaction and personal fulfillment or frustration and despair. With retirement from jobs and children launched into careers and marriage, the older adult years have brought us more leisure and longer blocks of time to be together.

✓ More time together is welcomed by couples who have continued to grow through the years with common interests and emotional closeness. If the marriage has been a good one, it can improve in old age if partners continue to be open to one another, willing to forget and forgive weaknesses and minor irritations, and are committed to grant to one another freedom to achieve his or her unique personhood.

The older adult years, however, will become a frightening vacuum with nothing to fill them for those husbands and wives who have allowed themselves to grow apart and become embittered. Now it becomes too easy to blame one another for what has happened in the past and cannot now be changed. Communication gradually breaks down, and each uses the other as an object on which to vent hostility and frustrations. The marriage relationship then becomes empty and devoid of meaning. Increased time together is filled with new frictions and resentments.

Many men and women during marriage have longed for more freedom from marital and child-rearing responsibilities to pursue their own interests. Conflicts, regrets, and deep hurts may have developed. Under pressure, when provoked, such a husband or wife has easily become angry, nagging, and unforgiving, and has even wondered at times if he or she should not have married someone else or even remained single. Now in these later years, as they look back, they can acknowledge to themselves and one another that, although each crisis brought its own pain and despair, out of each came a new understanding and closeness with one another. Now as mature adults they have achieved within their marriage relationship a priceless dimension of mutuality and trust.

REFLECTIONS ON

PATTERNS THAT CHANGE WHEN HUSBANDS RETIRE

Many wives remember well the sudden shift in daily routines when their husbands retired and no longer left home each

Figure 3. The need for love cannot be retired.

morning for jobs but began spending large portions of their now free time at home. Both then faced the necessity of learning how to use the increased time together in mutually satisfying ways, leaving one another space for privacy and independence with a growing dependence on one another.

How comfortable and acceptable these new patterns are for both husbands and wives depends on many things. Even though a woman may have been employed outside her home while married, the years after the children have left home are far less traumatic for her than for her husband. Even though her husband's retirement was by choice and welcomed, it was for him a kind of emotional and professional death. This is especially true of men who, during their working years, developed no interests other than those related to their jobs. Men who have been executives, supervisors, and foremen of other workers often develop authoritarian personalities. These acquired ways of behaving are not easily modified. Such men often try to compensate for their feelings of diminished usefulness by trying to control and manage household routines which have always been the responsibility of their wives. Resentment and confusion around their roles easily arise, and time and energy are spent in repressing the growing hostilities that each spouse begins to feel. This dilemma can easily be solved when joint decisions are made, clearly defining the areas of responsibility that each will carry. Also, much pressure on their wives can be released when husbands take part-time or volunteer jobs in which they can continue to use their managerial skills.

On the other hand, some men are so relieved to be out from under the pressures of highly competitive jobs that they slip, at least for a time, happily into activities that make no demands on them. They are content to putter around the house, fitting comfortably into nonthreatening household routines with increasing dependence on their wives. Men who are willing and encouraged by their wives to help with household tasks often experience a real sense of security and enjoyment of their new roles. However, if a woman has resented her husband's domination in earlier years, she may now use his strivings for greater dependence on her to make him feel guilty and unsure of his adequacy as a man and husband.

Among my friends, the couples whose married lives seem to reflect continuing feelings of mutuality are those whose total existence has not become focused exclusively on the husband-and-wife relationship. Their marriages seems to be a true partnership of equals in which each has the freedom to become more of his or her own unique self and to develop individual interests and friendships.

A Letter from My Sister Describes the Adjustment Problems of Some Retired Husbands

Jane is four years younger than her husband Tom who retired six months ago from his Civil Service position. She is a writer of children's books and needs time alone to do her work. This she had until Tom retired. In her recent letter she wrote,

> *Dear Sis,*
>
> Don't get me wrong. I love Tom as much as ever, but he has become impossible now that he is retired. I no longer have a minute to call my own. He's worse than Mary's little lamb. When I vacuum in the living room he's right there. If I go into the kitchen he follows me there. If I call a friend he stands in the doorway and listens to the conversation. I no longer have one minute to call my own. He even comes to my studio while I am writing to read his morning paper. There is no place in this big house where I can have any privacy. Today when I was getting ready to go to my monthly bridge luncheon he became very angry, accusing me of always going out and leaving him alone! Really, I'm just about to climb the wall! If only he had some interests of his own or would find a part-time or volunteer job. I'm going to encourage him to go to the Volunteer Bureau. Some youth-serving agency really needs him, I'm sure. He's too great a guy to settle for just being my shadow.
>
> And what are you up to these days? Do write soon.
>
> *Your loving sister, Jane.*

Jane's monthly bridge luncheon may not be her husband's favorite day in the month, but it shouldn't be such a calamity for Tom if he has enough interests to keep himself happily occupied and can still open the refrigerator door and use a can opener. Separate activities, interests, and friends can enliven conversations and life together. No interests or friends, however, should become so exclusive as to cause jealousies and suspicions between husbands and wives.

OBSERVATIONS ON

CHANGING ROLES WHEN HUSBANDS AND WIVES BECOME ILL

Mutually supportive marriage relationships inevitably break down when one becomes ill and increasingly dependent on the other. Since the chances are five times greater that husbands will die before their wives, many women must care for their ill husbands often over extended periods of time. Fears concerning the cost of the illness mount as finances become depleted. Resentment over the increasing responsibilities and lack of freedom and privacy develop, and wives begin to need assistance to overcome feelings of self-pity and martyrdom. How successful both mates will be in handling these new stresses will depend on how close and supportive they have been to one another during earlier crisis periods.

• Mrs. S. in these emotionally packed words told me of her experience in caring for her ill spouse: "The man who went to the hospital (following a stroke) never came home again. When they brought my husband home he couldn't talk, couldn't walk, couldn't feed himself, and he had a catheter attached to his penis. They just brought home this big lump that I brought back to life. But for six years I didn't have anyone to tell how hard it was to manage. Everybody talked about having a stiff upper lip and said, 'Oh, how brave and courageous you are,' but I didn't cry because nobody gave me the chance."

After a period of convalescence, Mr. S. was able to get around with the aid of a cane. For a few years he was able to participate in a limited way in activities. He greatly enjoyed the stimulation of classes at the nearby college. Recently his physical condition began deteriorating again, and now he has to be in a wheel chair most of the time. Mrs. S.'s health is not really good, and she is too frail to manage lifting either him or the wheelchair into a car. His motivation for getting out from their home was decreased as the difficulties in doing so have increased.

When I visited with Mrs. S. recently she again shared her frustrations:

> You can't imagine the feeling of freedom in having a few hours or a day to myself when a friend occasionally takes Sam out for a while. Most of the time, though, he sits in the middle of the living room with his feet up on the footstool, and he's a very heavy presence even though I love him dearly. To say that I don't miss sex with Sam would be far from the truth. His emotions as well as his body seem paralyzed. He'll hug, but there's no feeling in it. And just hugging, whew!! So even though we attempted for a while to maintain intercourse, the damage to his brain and his sensitivity was such that we finally stopped trying. It's no wonder that I become incredibly ill at the end of ten years after caring for Sam physically and emotionally with no return for me. It was not the loss of the sex act itself that was so deadening; it's the intensity of the yearning and loving that still persists and Sam's inability to respond in any way.

After enduring a series of illnesses and injuries which she called "accidentititis" — breaking a wrist and three ribs and developing a hiatal hernia — she told me that she had tried suicide more than once through pill overdoses, but, fortunately, she never succeeded. Finally, she sought counseling, and she says it has literally saved her life, but she still feels the frustration of the day-to-day burdensome chores of attending a once vital man who is now a mere husk of himself. "I need privacy, the chance to be alone in my own environment or to go away for a day or two to a conference or workshop," Mrs. S. explained.

She is cognizant too of the fact that her husband's needs are just as varied and great as hers. She has looked in vain for an intellectually stimulating environment where her husband might go for a few hours each day. "When he was in the college campus he loved so much I was uneasy at first, but I knew the kids looked after him when he was there. They are so beautiful. I always knew he was safe because they enjoyed taking this old bearded sea captain around and taking care of him."

The centrally located senior center in the county is of no interest to either of them since bingo, card playing, and other activities offered there are not sufficient stimulation. Furthermore, there he meets other windy old men like himself who all have stories they want to tell, and there's no one to listen. Mrs. S. says he needs someone to listen to him, play chess with him, and motivate him to keep exercising. "People try to help you on their terms and not on the basis of our needs. Social workers tend to set up their idea of what somebody needs and then lay it on them. If Sam doesn't try to keep walking, he will end up in a nursing home, and God forbid that!" she exclaimed somewhat apprehensively.

• Anna R.'s husband also has been severely damaged by a stroke suffered some years ago, and his difficulties are compounded by a loss of hearing. She tells her story in these words:

> I get into terrible depressions; it's almost indescribable. That person (my husband) is a constant reminder that he no longer functions well physically. While both of us agree that we function quite well mentally, no matter how old one is he needs encouragement to use his faculties. Until last year I could go away for as long as a week for a visit, but not anymore. He fell recently and hurt his spine, and we don't know to what extent this will affect him. He is not unpleasant when he is sick; he loves it in a way. He doesn't want me to go out, but I just tell him that he can't tell me what to do and where to go. We are in the process of exhausting our funds, and Medicare is still very inadequate.

Anna thinks the state should use more of its resources to provide home care, although she places an even higher value on obtaining an attendant to get her husband out for a few hours each day, which would benefit both of them. They get an occasional letter from their children, but the only support these children have to offer is the admonition for them to "take good care of yourselves."

• I hope many communities will develop programs similar to those my friend Mollie told me about in her last letter. Between the lines of her previous one I had detected her depression and emotional exhaustion from the increasing responsibilities of caring for her husband, Ray, who had been left partially paralyzed after a severe stroke last winter. Her recent letter was so cheerful and full of hope. She wrote,

Dear Florence:

You haven't heard from me lately, and I'm truly sorry. I just haven't had the energy or anything of interest to write. All of my time and so much of me is spent these days in caring for and being with Ray. I have been feeling completely drained and dried up! But something truly wonderful has happened in Westville. We now have a Senior Day Care Center, and what a difference it is making in our lives. Here frail and handicapped individuals may spend the day. This gives their spouses, or others who care for them, a bit of a breather and a break from responsibilities which so many times weigh so heavily. Two times a week Ray is called for and taken, wheelchair and all, in a mini-bus to the Center where he spends the day from 10 to 3 o'clock. There, under a specially trained staff, who understand the feelings and frustrations of stroke victims, he enjoys playing table games, attends a speech therapy group, and has a good hot meal at noon. Best of all, though, he escapes from our four walls where he has virtually been a prisoner for the past ten months. At the Center he sees new faces and finds new interests. I know something really good happens to him for he seems more like his old self when he returns home. And what about me, you ask? To have five hours two days a week totally for myself is the most wonderful feeling imaginable. Some days I just rest and read! I even went to town the other day for lunch and attended a meeting of my church circle. A greatly needed change!

Now I hear there are plans to develop a Respite Center in the abandoned wing of one of our hospitals. This will mean that children who care for their aging parents, or someone like myself, can plan for their care there and get away for a needed vacation. I'm not at all sure now that I would take advantage of this and go away, but to know that I can makes such a difference. Now I often find myself thinking that no matter how hard Ray's care becomes and how discouraged I get, there is help. I feel so relieved and supported by the counsellors at the center and no longer feel alone.

I wanted you to know how much better I am feeling and how much brighter life looks. Ray joins me in sending our fondest wishes to you.

Mollie

OBSERVATIONS ON

PERSONALITY CHANGES IN OLDER MEN AND WOMEN

I have frequently been aware of a reversal of personality traits in many married couples as they grow older. According to Jungian psychology we each have qualities of the other sex within us, not only in the biological sense that our glands secrete both male and female hormones, but also we each have inherited certain archetypal ideas of what the other sex is like. Since we experience strong social pressures to conform to cultural definitions of "maleness" and "femininity," and "anima" (female traits in men) and "animus" (male traits in women) remain unexpressed. The renowned psychiatrist, Karl Jung, believed that the second half of life is compensatory for the first, and that each sex in the later years lives out and enjoys some of the qualities that had been conceded to the other. Sharp sex distinctions of earlier adulthood break down, and each sex becomes to some degree what the other used to be. Men in their later years no longer fear their masculinity is threatened in expressing their anima traits. They become more gentle and affable, more submissive and dependent. Likewise, women no longer feel inhibited in expressing their animus feelings. Women who have always been nurturing, receptive, and sensitive, in old age often become self-confident, tough-minded, and decisive in their relationships with their husbands. Personality traits that formerly caused mates to be critical of one another and even openly hostile, in old age become not only acceptable but even endearing.

REFLECTIONS ON

SEXUALITY IN THE LATER YEARS

We have long been saddled in our society with the myth that love and romance are only for the young, for those with strong and beautiful bodies, with skin not yet sagging and wrinkled. Now headlines on newspaper features and magazine articles proclaim that sex is O.K. for the old as well. This openness to the fact that older people have continuing sexual needs and interests is a natural spin-off of the more relaxed attitudes around sex in our present culture. Recent studies of successful adjustment patterns of the older adult personality affirm that their continuing interest in one another as sexual partners is not only normal and possible but is also a positive and healthy component of the physical and emotional aging process. Preconditioned by strict Victorian attitudes, many older people feel that to show interest in sex is not normal. They have too easily accepted the myth that such interest is terminated early in the sixth decade and that the physical exertion involved in the sexual act is in fact dangerous to health. As our whole society moves into a period of greater realism and more tolerant attitudes around human sexuality, it will become easier for old people, too, to talk honestly and freely about sexual feelings and experiences.

I remember well how high some eyebrows were raised back in 1950 when the findings of the pioneer study by Dr. Kinsey on human sexuality were first released. Subsequent studies by Dr. William Masters and Virginia Johnson substantiated his findings and also affirmed that, although sexual interests and capacities slow down as one ages, they need not end. In their interviews of older adults, Masters and Johnson found that an active sex life was still being enjoyed by many men and women in their seventies and eighties and even until the ninth decade, if they were in good health and had always had an active sex life. Continuing intimacy, tenderness, and touching — all provide needed psychological reinforcements when the woman's physical attractiveness and the man's sense of adequacy begin to wane.

Longitudinal studies on the sexual practices of a group of 250 older men and women from sixty to ninety-four years of age have been carried on at the Center for Aging and Human Behavior at Duke University since 1950. The findings show that patterns of sexual interest and modes of expression differ substantially within the group. Coital activity continues for some, while others have learned that sexual satisfaction does not necessarily depend on coitus. Almost 80 percent of the men as compared with 30 percent of the women reported continuing sexual interests. The smaller percentage of the women sexually active was due to a lack of suitable sex partners and their greater reluctance, in contrast to men, to participate in non-marital sex. These proportions did not change significantly in a follow-up study made ten years later.

I recently read some statistics that startled me. In the older adult population today there are over 10 million widows and only 2 million widowers. This is due to the fact that the probability that their mates will die before they do is five times greater for women than for men. With this disproportionate distribution of older women over men, the active sex life of many older women must terminate at the death of their spouses, since a younger man as a sex partner for an older women is generally socially disapproved, and she is thought deviant if she expresses sexual interest outside of marriage.

I remember so clearly a conversation I had with a close friend when we were both nearing our menopausal years. She confessed to me that lately things had grown a bit strained and tense between her and her husband. She was experiencing, for no obvious reason, recurring mood swings between euphoria and deep depression. Her doctor had finally prescribed a program of hormonal therapy. All during this time she told me her husband seemed so depressed and noncommunicative. "Finally," she confided, "I determined to talk with him about how impossible he was behaving and how uncomfortable and unhappy he was making me feel." Then, with a noticeable lightness in her voice, she said, "Jack finally told me that the reason he was feeling so distraught and anxious was because he thought that with the beginning of the menopause we could no longer enjoy sex. I had to confess to him that I was really looking forward to the menopause, for then we could have sex without my worrying about becoming pregnant."

Many husbands are not as fortunate as Jack. Women who have never fully adjusted to the physical aspects of marriage use the menopause as an excuse to cease all sexual activity. They thus create for their husbands and themselves serious problems.

Although important physiological changes occur in the female body which make it no longer possible for her to bear children after the menopause, women do remain fully capable of sexual performances at orgasmic response levels. The only change seems to be in the rapidity and intensity of her response to erotic stimulation. There is no clinical evidence that men experience changes similar to those of the woman, although there is a loss of sex steroids similar to the woman's loss of estrogen.

The declining ability of some older men to maintain a high level of sexual functioning is very often due to psychological rather than physical factors. Anxiety and stress around possible impotency, increasing boredom with a wife who fails to maintain her physical attractiveness, and the fear of sudden death during intercourse from a heart attack or stroke — all affect a man's sense of adequacy and sexual potency. Studies made of sudden deaths during intercourse remain inconclusive, though the medical profession affirm that such deaths occur much less frequently than patients fear. Problems of hypertension and cardiovascular accidents in older individuals do often call for some readjustment in sexual practices, but a habit of total abstinence, according to the medical profession, cannot be justified.

Certain chronic conditions sometimes develop in the reproductive system of the aging body which necessitate hysterectomies in women and prostate surgery in men. Again doctors affirm that these surgeries do not terminate sexual desire or performance in either men or women. As long as both partners remain interesting to one another and they anticipate an active sex life, there is no reason why they will not be able to continue to grow in a deepening appreciation and enjoyment of one another in this important aspect of our humanness.

SOME OBSERVATIONS ON

THE EXPERIENCE OF WIDOWHOOD

My friend Meg's letter which arrived not long ago is typical of so many that I receive with greater and greater frequency these days. I had written Meg a note expressing my concern and sympathy after receiving a telephone call from her daughter informing me of her father's heart attack and sudden death. Meg's letter is such a valiant attempt to express the feelings that I know have engulfed her since then:

> *Dear Florence,*
>
> Your thoughtful note was so comforting and helpful during those hectic days following John's death and funeral. I planned to write sooner but I simply haven't been able to cope with the shock and emptiness that have left me feeling so numb and alone. The children were able to stay with me for a week following the funeral, but, of course, they had to return to their jobs and families. I can't describe how frightened I feel now. I must finally accept the reality of John's death and begin to sort out my feelings and face the necessity of living my life without him. There are times when I think that I won't make it.
>
> It's hard to say, but sometimes I even feel angry that he has left me alone with so many problems to face. My days seem to be haunted with the thought that perhaps there were things I could have done to protect him. I know now that I should have insisted that he see his doctor when he complained of being so tired after our trip across the country last summer. Now I know that trip was too strenuous, and I am feeling so guilty that I kept insisting that we take it. My loneliness is only intensified by the frustration that I now feel in being so ignorant and helpless about all of the financial and legal matters that now face me. Well-meaning friends and relatives are trying to advise me, but I know that I must make my own decisions.
>
> It has really helped me to write so frankly to you. I wish that this visit might have been in person, but that will have to

wait until I am feeling more calm and settled. I do appreciate your understanding love and concern for me.

Meg.

Meg's letter seemed to cry out for a response, and I wrote her the following day:

Dear Meg:

I want you to know how good it was to hear from you and to have you write so honestly about your feelings around John's death. I truly salute you that you are able to mourn and write about your feelings. Don't feel guilty because you feel angry to be left alone with so many hard problems to face. Anger and fear may not seem like socially approved ways to express sadness and grief, but let me reassure you that they are perfectly normal responses to the loss of one on whom you have depended for so many years. I'm sure that you will never forget John and the good life that you had together, but the acceptance of his death will become easier as you begin to adjust to your new roles and responsibilities. It will not be easy for you to find again that important part of you that was lost when John died and to realize yourself again as a whole person, responsible to yourself alone, but I know you can do it. Let me know how it goes.

I heard recently from another friend who too has lost her husband and is experiencing the same lost feelings as you. She wrote that she was getting so much help from a widow's club which she has joined. She said that sharing her feelings and fears with other women who had had like experiences gave her new insights and a great sense of support. I wonder if there is such a group in your community. It might be worth exploring.

I so hope that you can come to California this winter for a visit. We need some long talks together.

Always my love,
Florence.

The loss of a life mate with whom the ties through life have been close and supportive is one of life's most devastating experiences. One cannot generalize that it is more traumatic for one spouse than for the other, for there are many different factors that operate in the lives of men and women. The adjustment, however, is frequently made easier for women, for they have maintained throughout life a closer contact with their children and grandchildren and other relatives. Furthermore, a woman is spared the experience that is so overwhelming to so many men of being responsible for the first time in their lives to care for themselves, to manage a home, shop, and prepare meals. For these reasons there are really more benefits for men than for women in remarrying. In addition to a wife, a man again has a homemaker and cook, as well as a hostess and a companion for life.

On the other hand, men do not necessarily experience the same social isolation as women on the loss of their spouses. They have been more accustomed to socialize informally with other men on the street corner, on the bus, in the bar, at sport events, and in lodge, union, and fraternal halls. A man continues to be welcome in social groups that he and his wife had participated in together. He is not a threat to anyone but a welcomed "extra man" for many social affairs.

For a woman it is different. Continuing as a member of a social group that she and her husband had enjoyed together serves as a constant reminder that she is now alone. She feels vulnerable, uncomfortable, and insecure. Soon she either refuses invitations or is dropped by her former friends because of the difficulty of planning an escort and transportation for her. If she is an attractive widow, outgoing and friendly, she becomes an unconscious threat to other women in the group. In time she drops out of mixed social groups and moves socially only with other women who also have lost their spouses and are lonely.

Many women when they become widowed experience a new sense of themselves as independent persons and welcome again the freedom to make their own decisions and be responsible only for themselves. This is especially true for a woman who has cared for an ill husband for a long period of time and experiences during her widowhood the sense of being a whole person and not just half of a couple. Another widow might choose to remain single, believing that she could never find another spouse who could measure up to the one she has lost, and her memories are too happy and precious to be supplanted

by another.

OBSERVATIONS ON

REMARRIAGE AMONG WIDOWED OLDER ADULTS

After a period of mourning and living alone, some individuals decide that life is more satisfying if they can experience the continuing emotional support and companionship of other persons. Since the myth that love and romance are only for the young has been exploded, I am becoming increasingly aware of second marriages among many older adults who have lost their life partners. United States Census figures show that the number of brides sixty-five years and older increased from 7800 in 1960 to 16,400 in 1973.

Although there are many strong arguments for the remarriage of widowed men and women after an appropriate period of mourning, some very practical problems have arisen in the lives of several of my friends. I remember especially the rough experience of my neighbor, Frank. Almost two years after losing his wife, Frank met an attractive and congenial widow at a senior center which he attended regularly to fill some of his times of loneliness. When he wrote his son and daughter who lived in a nearby state of his intention to remarry, they both arrived on an unannounced visit. It was hard for them, I am sure, to realize how lonely their father was or to accept the fact that, even though he was seventy, it was quite normal for him to have sexual interests and feel the need for the companionship of a warm, loving human being. His children seemed to feel that for him to remarry would be disloyal to their mother, and neither seemed to be able to adjust his or her emotions to welcome a new member into the family. Their hostility and strong opposition subsided, however, after Frank explained to them that he had had his lawyer draw up a marital contract in which he and his new wife would both agree that they would maintain their own separate bank accounts, their individual estates would remain intact, and their previous wills valid.

It was a different story for Ned. His wife had been an invalid for almost ten years before her death. His children had urged him many time to come East and live near or with one of them. Although desperately lonely, he had resisted their repeated invitations, saying that he felt that it would be unwise for him to leave all his long-time friends and the community where he had lived all of his life. Eventually, a high school sweetheart, who too had been widowed, returned to the community to live with her sister. She and Ned soon renewed their acquaintance and decided to marry. His children received the news with relief and recognized that they would no longer experience so much concern and anxiety about his welfare and loneliness. They were grateful that there would again be someone to assume responsibility for his care and happiness. Ned's story is being repeated many times over as widowed men and women are able to make new affectional relationships in the multipurpose senior centers, retirement communities, senior citizens' travel clubs, and community-sponsored luncheon and social centers.

When men remarry it is usually after three years of widowhood, and then they choose younger wives. They are thus able to put the reality of death farther away in their consciousnesses. If women remarry it is more often after a longer period of widowhood. The most successful remarriages that I have observed have been between individuals of similar social, economic, and religious backgrounds. Many times such couples have known one another in their youth, been friends with their respective first spouses, or were members of the same church or social group. With the encouragement of their children and friends they remarry mainly for companionship. However, if either the husband or the wife has not been able to work through his grief and indulges in unfavorable comparisons between his new spouse and an idealized version of the former, a remarriage can become a devastating and totally unhappy experience. Important decisions as to where they will live, how they will manage their individual and joint incomes, who will pay which bills, and what activities and interests they will enjoy together in order to grow as interesting people — these all will help to insure a happy second marriage.

According to the 1965 United States Census Bureau, over

26,000 older couples are making an alternative choice of living together without legal marriage. This figure is thought to be an understatement of the actual number. The sexual freedom and alternative marriage patterns that have been allowed to younger and middle aged adults have even greater rationale for members of the older generation, based on economic factors alone. As of late 1977, since benefits from pensions, Social Security, Supplemental Security Income, and eligibility for food stamps are affected when recipient status is formally changed by marriage, many couples actually can not afford to enter into a legal contract. Some have a church ceremony to celebrate the event but do not formalize it with a marriage certificate. Such arrangements have many positive advantages, including the security of a home, the reinstatement of the integrity and self-esteem inherent in the husband and wife roles, ready peer companionship, and if desired, a partner for sex. These can be assured without financial and legal complications or lasting commitments should it prove to be a misalliance.

SOME OBSERVATIONS ON

DIVORCE

Most divorces occur during earlier life periods, but the survival of a marriage into a late life is not necessarily an indication that it has been a successful and happy one. Many men and women seem to arrive at their older adults years completely beaten down by a succession of life experiences that have left them disillusioned, unsure of themselves and their self-worth. If their marriage, too, has been allowed to become monotonous and meaningless, they often seem immobile and unable to take any creative steps to revitalize or terminate that marriage or perhaps to make a new one. Such couples settle for a kind of moratorium in their marriage but continue to live under the same roof, often with continual bickering or with no communication or mutual caring. There are sometimes situations where the wife has been an invalid for many years and was unable to be a marriage partner. When the husband of an invalid wife is unwilling or reluctant to dissolve the marriage, he often enters into an extramarital relationship with the full knowledge of his mate. Although extramarital relationships in some situations are understandable and increasingly acceptable in our society, they continue to be circumspect and generally frowned on by most older adults today who were reared in a time when all but monogamous legal marriages were considered shocking and sinful.

As marriage patterns in modern America become increasingly fluid and innovative, those among older adults will reflect the changes. What models will eventually find general acceptance is not yet clear, but of one thing we are certain; companionship, sex, love, romance, and marriage for older men and women are continuing needs and cannot be retired.

Chapter 5

ALL IN THE FAMILY — INCLUDING THE THIRD AND FOURTH GENERATIONS

> Let there be space in your to-getherness,
> The souls of your children dwell in the house of tomorrow,
> Which you cannot visit, even in your dreams,
> You may strive to be like them, but seek not to make
> them like you.
> For life goes not backward nor tarries with yesterday.
>
> *The Prophet* BY KAHLIL GIBRAN*

"I'M determined never to be a burden on my children or impose on them in any way." Why do so many of us voice such resolute determination when we talk together about our fears and plans for the future? We reassure ourselves and others that it is not because our children show a lack of love or concern for us. Life-long ties of affection and loyalty are not that easily broken. No, I believe these attitudes reflect rather our determination to continue to be independent and in charge of our own lives for as long as possible. According to a recent national survey, nine out of ten of us over sixty-five hold these attitudes. There are many reasons why this is true that are primarily due to basic changes in the structure and function of the family and the changing roles and relationships of the older generation within it.

Like so many of our social institutions, the family is being stretched into new shapes by demands and pressures inherent in our permissive, urban, technological society. Today's family is made up of multiple units. Four out of ten of us live in households headed by one of our adult children. The majority of us,

*Reprinted from *The Prophet*, by Kahlil Gibran, with permission of the publisher, Alfred A. Knopf, Inc. Copyright 1923 by Kahlil Gibran; renewal copyright 1951 by Administrators C.T.A. of Kahlil Gibran Estate, and Mary G. Gibran.

however, live independently in our own households, in a satellite relationship to the core family, composed of the adult child and his/her spouse and children. An interdependency exists between us, with an ongoing interchange of visiting, shopping, holiday celebrations, financial aid, care when ill, and other services. This pattern of living independently of our children does not mean that we have been forsaken by them. Doctor Ethel Shanas at the National Opinion Research Center of the University of Chicago found in a recent study that among those of us who live successfully in the community, the majority live in close proximity to one or more of our children. Three out of ten of us live within ten minutes or less from one of our children, and only 7 percent live farther than two hours away. Over two thirds of us see one of our sons or daughters at least weekly. Airplanes and automobiles bring us together with other family members in a relatively short time. The telephone company assures us that "your family is as near as your nearest phone," and the time is not too far distant when, with the video-phone, we will be able to see them as well as hear their voices. Studies of how close many of us live to our children are reassuring when the old stereotype persists that we are alone and abandoned by them. These studies, however, tell nothing about the quality of the relations of adult children who live near their aging parents. We should not conclude that physical proximity necessarily brings emotional closeness.

REFLECTIONS ON

CHOICES OF HOW WE WILL LIVE

Our parents and grandparents had no choice but to live with their children or other relatives when they became widowed or ill. We do have a choice! Many programs and services have been developed to make it possible and even preferable in some situations for an older person to live alone. There are sources of income open to us now which our parents never had: annuities, Social Security, Supplemental Security Income, and veteran's benefits. We also have options of where we will live and how.

Figure 4. All in the family — the first and fourth generations.

Many of us will continue to live in the homes where we have raised our families and will rent our extra rooms to students or share with other older persons in order to meet the cost of upkeep on the property and higher taxes. Other options include senior citizens' housing projects financed by federal, state, and local government funds; retirement communities built and sponsored by churches, lodges, and other nonprofit groups; retirement hotels, condominiums, and mobile home parks where we can live without responsibilities for maintenance. These all give us welcomed choices at rents many of us are able to afford. Medicare and Medi-Cal help pay our medical and hospital bills, and visiting nurses, home-health aides, chore services, and hot meals delivered to our homes help us to remain independent of our children, even when we are ill. These community-based services are an affirmation that society has accepted some responsibility, along with our children, when we need help. This is good!

REFLECTIONS ON

THE RESPONSIBILITY OF CHILDREN FOR THEIR AGED PARENTS

Traditional attitudes of previous generations demanded not only respect but also care for aged parents, even though it necessitated sacrifices from the next generation. Today parents are expected to give to their children, and their children are expected to reciprocate, not by giving back to their parents but by giving to their own children. This idea is beautifully expressed in an old Hebrew legend (source unknown):

> There once was an eagle which set out to cross a windy sea with his fledging. The sea was so wide and the wind so strong that the father bird was forced to carry his young one in his claws. When he was halfway across, the wind turned to a gale and he said, "My child, look how I am struggling and risking my life in your behalf. When you are grown will you do as much for me and provide for me in my old age?"
>
> "My dear father," the eaglet replied, "it is true that you are struggling mightily and risking your life in my behalf, and I

> shall be wrong not to repay you when you are grown old. I cannot, however, at this critical time bind myself. This though, I can promise, when I am grown and have children of my own, I shall do as much for them as you have done for me.

There is a concern in our society that a growing irresponsibility and lack of respect exists on the part of too many adult children for their aging parents. Emotional closeness between parents and children is not something that we can take for granted. How close this relationship is in old age is determined by the quality of the relationship during earlier life periods. A grown child may love his parents but still harbor resentment and hostility from childhood injustices, real or imagined. If there were open conflicts and misunderstandings then, the hurts will still be deeply felt by both parents and children. Parents may both love and resent adult children — resent because they can no longer control their children, and because their roles are now in fact reversed. Adult children too often try to take over and make decisions for their parents. They mean well, but they often manage too much! It should help to ease the guilt and discomfort that we often feel concerning relations with our children to know that such negative feelings are common to us all. If, on the other hand, our relations with our children throughout the years have been ones of mutual love and concern, then these loving feelings continue and grow even stronger. But if, because of illness or some other crisis, our dependency on our children increases and our needs place a greater demand on their financial and emotional resources than they can or should be expected to carry, then feelings between our adult children and ourselves may become strained.

OBSERVATIONS ON

THREE-GENERATIONAL LIVING

So many questions about the wisdom of living with our children and their families are raised these days that many of us, when we do live with our children, feel that we must justify our decisions. My friend Elizabeth, I am sure, was needing to be reassured when she wrote me the following letter:

Dear Florence,

You may be surprised to learn that I have finally made the decision to sell my home and move to New York to live with my daughter Jane and her family. As you know, I have not been well since John died and have been considering this move for several years. I have been so relieved that Jane has not made unrealistic demands on me or pressured me to make this decision before I was ready. I have taken time to look thoughtfully, and I hope wisely, at my own needs as well as my ability to live here alone. Now I have made my decisions and I feel really good about it.

I decided that I didn't want to become a stubborn, unreasonable old lady, maintaining my own home and lifestyle when it placed more demands on my children than was fair for me to make. I love Jane and Jack too much to add unnecessarily to their anxiety and concern for me in living so far from them, and I certainly do not want them, in the future, to feel guilty thinking they neglected me. I am not fooling myself. I know there will be misunderstandings, times of deep loneliness and doubt that I made the right decision, but I will have to cope with those feelings when they come. Now I want, above all, to be able to live my days in their home in dignity and with all the grace and contentment I can muster. I shall hate myself if I become a demanding mother and carping grandmother, creating stress and tensions in their lives and draining them of their patience and love. I only hope that they will respect my need for privacy and will give me the freedom to be me. This I shall also want to grant them.

It has helped me to share these thoughts with you. Be sure to call me when you come to New York. I'm in the phone book! I'll meet you for lunch!

All my best to you,
Elizabeth

How wonderful it would be if we were all as emotionally mature and thoughtful of our children as Elizabeth. And why can't all children be as wise and patient as Jane in letting us have the time and freedom to make our own difficult decisions, I wonder! There will be many times in the days ahead, I am sure, when Elizabeth will be discouraged, and Jane's patience will be put to the test. The adjustments that both must make in living again in one household with the parent-child roles reversed will not be easy after living apart fifty years or more! Children, even when adults, still know their parents only in the role of parents. To accept one's parent as persons in their own right with their own interests and needs is often difficult for adult children.

Although the success of living with children will depend on a mutual interchange of personal favors and goodwill, there are many practical considerations that should be faced before the decision is made. How do you and your adult children honestly feel about one another? Are you mutually supportive, cooperative, and respectful, or resentful, critical, and openly antagonistic? Do your children's spouses share these attitudes? Will you be accepted by your child's spouse, or will you become the battleground on which they will act out their interpersonal hostilities and incompatibilities? Has there been a clear understanding of what responsibilities, if any, you shall have for the care and discipline of your grandchildren? If your daughter or daughter-in-law works outside the home, are you able and willing to take over some of the management of the home, or will you feel imposed upon? Have decisions been made about what living space will be yours, and is it agreed that it will give you the privacy and independence that you need? Have decisions been made about sharing household expenses? When differences and misunderstandings arise will you be able to be open and honest about the things that bother you, or will you clam up and console yourself with self-pity? Can you adjust, without becoming judgmental, to behavior that may be distasteful to you but which is acceptable and a part of the value system and lifestyle of the younger generation? Have you faced the necessity of having your own friends and social life so that your child and his or her family can have times for being together without you?

Initial resolutions to be a considerate, cooperative member of the home of one of your children may soon give way to feelings of martyrdom and alienation. Personal traits and little habits which parents have acquired over the years often, under tension, annoy their children. Sharp criticism and confrontations over matters of minor importance follow. The sensitive older person begins to feel that he is the cause and target of tensions and hostilities which are, in fact, normal occurrences in all family living. In such situations the stresses and strains of three-generational living soon begin to overshadow the joys and satisfactions.

Again there are no good guys or villians in this family drama, only parents and their adult children, each with different needs, perceptions, and goals. Each needs to pay attention to the other. An understanding friend or counsellor, who can listen objectively and interpret what is happening as the older parent begins to act out his frustrations and dependency needs, can be of great help to the adult child as well as be a confidant and offer support to the troubled older person. Sometimes problems become too critical and difficult to handle, and a joint decision for out-of-home care may be the best solution both for the younger family as well as the older parent.

Further Observations on

Three- and Four-Generational Living

Many parents decide that their relations with their adult children will be more satisfactory if they do not live with them, as they have been independent too long to want to give up the freedom and control over their own lives. A woman who has lived in a dependency relationship to men all of her life, to father, boss, and husband, might be reluctant as a widow to move into the home of a child and be dependent on her son or son-in-law. Other parents may choose to live independently because of emotional distances and unspoken tensions between themselves and their children which date back many years. Human relations and emotions are complex, and long-standing feelings of not being understood and the inability to communicate with parents are not easily overcome by children. One often hears parents complain, "Just see how my children treat me after all I have done for them." Have you ever voiced such complaints? We need to remember that we will receive the love of our children only if it is an expression of their true feelings, not because they consider it a duty.

How insensitively and thoughtlessly we respond sometimes to our children's and grandchildren's expressions of love. A friend told me recently about a surprise party her children and grandchildren had given to celebrate her seventy-fifth birthday. I was shocked when she said, "When I got home I got the stepladder and put all of the presents on the top shelf of the closet. I'll never use all of those things." True, we often feel so surfeited with things! We are trying to get rid of what we have rather than to accumulate more! But when children and grandchildren care enough to remember us on our special days, we need to be appreciative and receptive. Of course they feel hurt when we don't use their gifts! The problem usually lies in us. It is so difficult to receive graciously from those to whom we have always been the giver. As we grow older we need to learn how to receive with some degree of grace without whining about "paying you back." Children and grandchildren are often at their wit's end about what to give us. How wise we would be to have ready some suggestions of expendable items we could use, such as a plant, a book, a ticket for a play or concert, or, better still, a kiss and a hug.

However close we are to our children we will many times feel an overpowering sense of loneliness. Then we find ourselves reaching out in emotionally unhealthy ways to try to tighten our hold on their affections. It is difficult to develop a sense of detachment from our children. We often try unwisely to remain too involved in their lives and interests and become critical of their spouses, how they run their homes, and how they discipline their children. Such interference by us inevitably leads to resentment. We place too heavy an emotional burden on our children when we focus all of our time and interest on them, deciding that they and their attention is all that we have left in life. It will be difficult but essential to free ourselves from too great a dependency on them if we are concerned about their mental health and well-being. Our primary responsibility is no longer to our children but to ourselves.

REFLECTIONS ON

BEING A MOTHER-IN-LAW

Relationships with our sons-in-law and daughters-in-law can be among the most satisfying and supportive of our older adult years. For some of us, however, this relationship with the spouses of our adult children can bring heartaches and disappointments. The relationship between mothers and daughters-in-law seems especially fraught with tensions and misunderstandings.

I have known for a long time that my friend Ruth was having a rough time in doing what she described as "her part" in keeping her relations with her daughter-in-law harmonious and on an even keel. She had always kept her son Allen, an only child whose father had died when he was a teenager, very dependent on her. I have a sneaking suspicion that Ruth unconsciously resented Sue for, as she expressed it, "taking my son away from me." Ruth had talked herself into believing that because Sue's parents had been able to give their daughter many social and cultural opportunities, Sue's expectations and demands on Allen would be more than he, with a modest salary, could meet. Ruth early developed the self-defeating attitude that she had little in common with Sue and therefore no hope of ever having a mutually comfortable and caring intimacy with her. Her words and actions have not helped to bridge the gap. I have never heard her say, "Allen and Sue." She refers to them as "my son Allen and his wife." She fails to recognize that Allen's first loyalty now is to Sue. Ruth's demands on her son's time and attention seem unreasonable and her criticism of Sue thoughtless. Thus a constant state of misunderstandings and hurt feelings persists.

Ruth's relations with Sue are not unique. Normal stresses and competitive feelings between young women and their mothers-in-law are common human experiences. The age difference itself can cause jealousy in some older women. They may envy and resent the youth, gaiety, and vigor of their daughters-in-law as they enter one of life's happiest and most productive periods. Many older women also believe and often express their concerns that their daughters-in-law are simply not qualified or capable of caring for their sons and, in time, their grandchildren. Unless she is demonstrably warm and supportive, a mother-in-law can pose an ever present threat to the daughter-in-law, who may view the mother-in-law as a super woman, whose homemaking and social skills she will never be able to achieve.

I have known young couples for whom any real or imagined shortcomings of one another have triggered, under the normal pressures of marriage and family life, criticisms of their respective parents. Such gibes as, "If you hadn't been so spoiled, you would be more thoughtful of me," or "If your mother had trained you well, you would know that you should call me when you expect to be late for dinner." The husband may say, "Too bad your mother didn't help you with homemaking skills." Such remarks may be made in a good-natured way, but they raise negative feelings and imply criticisms of the other's parents that may grow.

To say that in-laws should never give advice or make suggestions would be unrealistic and take the spontaneity out of relationships with married children. Many times an open, honest expression of one's true feelings can clear the air. It takes time and patience to discover when and on what subjects suggestions will be welcomed by our adult children.

Close relationships between both sets of parents of a married couple can also add enrichment and happiness as we share together our grandchildren and meet at family celebrations. These relationships, however, can be destructive and disruptive if both sets of parents compete for the time and control of the young couple and the affection and attention of their grandchildren.

Although they are normal in many in-law relationships, stress and competition can be reduced if handled wisely by both generations. Close, mutually supportive, and satisfying relations can then result, adding new dimensions and satisfactions to all those involved.

OBSERVATIONS ON

THE ROLE AND STATUS OF ELDERLY PARENTS IN ETHNIC FAMILIES

Doctor James Lee, a pediatrician, his wife Susan, who teaches art in the high school, and their twin sons, juniors in high school, are our next-door neighbors. Not long ago, Doctor Lee's mother arrived from Hong Kong to make her home with him and his family. Realizing that Mrs. Lee must often feel strange and lonely, since all of the family members leave home early in the morning and do not return until late afternoon, I have often walked down to "visit" with her when I have seen her in the yard watering the garden. Our visits consist of warm smiles and a clasp of hands, since Mrs. Lee cannot speak English and I do not speak Chinese. Weekends seem to be such happy times for her when her other children and their families arrive for visits. Grandmother Lee seems to be all smiles on these occasions, and I can imagine how proud she must be of all of her children who have achieved leadership positions in the Chinese community and church and in their various professions. It seems sad, though, that although her children and grandchildren speak Chinese when talking with her, at other times they talk together in English. They have adopted American ways and attitudes that are so strange and unfamiliar to her, and I am sure that she must often feel lonely and aware of the chasm that exists between her and her Americanized children. Mrs. Lee as the matriarch and highly respected elder of her family seems to be the symbol of all the ancient traditions and heritage of their Chinese culture.

In a recent session of my class the members were discussing how they could remain close to their children and grandchildren without becoming overly dependent on them. I can still see the look of puzzled bewilderment that came over Maria Domingo's face. Finally she found courage to speak in her not-yet-perfect English. "I no understand you Anglos. You say grandchildren not thoughtful, not dependable, not responsible, not good. Always you judge!" Then she hesitated as if she had said too much and then found her courage to continue. "Not the way with Chicanos. El respecto! I respect my kids, they respect me. I not critical, they not critical. Better so, no heartaches!"

Maria Domingo that day helped us all to realize the very special relationship that exists in most ethnic families between the older and the younger generations. America as a melting pot is not real to them. Ethnic-background young people strive to be good Americans, but they also want to know, in order to affirm their own lives, their own origins and traditional cultures. They respect and feel close to their grandparents, for it is through them that their own identity is known and established. Sometimes I wonder if those young families whose forefathers came long ago to make their homes in this new country haven't failed to claim a most significant and affirming force in their personal lives. Too many let their older family members get too far from the center of their lives and affections.

OBSERVATIONS ON

GRANDPARENT RITUALS

There is a special ritual for grandparents in our society; it opens with these words, "Have you seen the latest pictures of my grandchildren?" Then picture albums appear and snapshots of grandchildren and great-grandchildren are proudly displayed. No subject establishes such immediate and intimate communication between us as our grandchildren. We love to participate in this ritual, repeat their latest clever sayings, and show proof of their beauty.

Our roles and relationships to our grandchildren and great-grandchildren and their response to us change as they grow from infants to young adulthood. We often confess that we enjoy, indulge, and coddle them more than we did our own children when they were small. Perhaps we are more relaxed since we have no continuing responsibility for them. There seems often to be a special closeness that we and they feel for each other. This seems to be true for both grandparents, irrespective of sex, who are with their grandchildren often and play a nurturing role to them. For grandfathers this maternal role is an unfamiliar one, but it brings a new sense of pride and happiness to those men who are able to accept it.

A number of my friends have adopted a beautiful practice in inviting, on a regular schedule, one of their grandchildren to spend the weekend with them. Each child knows when his "special day" will be and that he may choose to which museum, park, shopping area, or movie he and his grandparents will go, what games they will play, and which of his favorite things to eat he may request and have without fail! What an opportunity such a plan provides to remain close to one's grandchildren! And what a meaningful experience for a child to be taken away from his brothers and sisters and be given the "only child" treatment, to be listened to, understood, and accepted as his own special self. Such an expression of love from grandparents helps to supplement that from parents and gives a child the security that he needs from caring adults in order to grow up with a good image of himself.

As grandchildren grow into adolescence and young adulthood, we soon become aware that we are investing more of our love and interest in them than they reciprocate. Their lives become so full that they have limited time for us among their many friends, activities, and interests. When we become overly possessive and demanding of them, they seem to withdraw and become unresponsive and even casual in their relations with us. Then we are apt to react by feeling hurt and ignored; we think them rude and thoughtless. At other times, however, we and our adolescent grandchildren seem closely drawn to one another in bonds of intuitive understanding, closer sometimes than those with their parents.

As grandchildren mature our roles become less functional and increasingly symbolic. We become a link joining our children and their children to past generation family members. This linkage gives their lives continuity and a sense of where they have come from. Through us cultural and religious values, and family customs and traditions are passed on. My neighbor told me recently how pleased she was when her oldest granddaughter asked if she could come the day before the family dinner on Christmas to watch her make the stuffing for the turkey according to an old family recipe. "There's no one that makes it quite like you," she told her grandmother.

We know now that our acceptance as valued and loved persons will not come automatically from grandchildren just because we are their grandparents. We must achieve this by remaining vital and intellectually alive. Only then can they honestly respect and love us. Whether we are aware of it or not, we serve as role models to our grandchildren and great-grandchildren, and their own attitudes about old age will be determined by how they see us, their grandparents, living and growing through these years.

REFLECTIONS ON

BROKEN HOMES AND STEP-GRANDPARENTS

It's this very special place that our grandchildren fill in our hearts that made this letter from my former neighbor, Julie Davis, so poignant.

> *Dear Florence,*
>
> And what's new with you these days? I've been completely submerged in family problems lately. You've known and loved us for so many years! I want to bring you up to date on all the goings-on in the Davis clan.
>
> You, of course, remember my Tom, that mischievous youngster who used to keep the whole neighborhood upset with all of his pranks. He's still at it! I don't know when I've been so disturbed. I'm sure I told you in my Christmas letter that he and Carol had divorced and that she had married one of their mutual college friends, a man with three children from a previous marriage. She has taken the children, Pat and Teddy, to New York where they will all live in his home on Long Island. A letter from Tom last week brought the news that he has met a divorcee whom he loves very much and that they plan to marry in June. She has four children. Image that!
>
> Somehow I feel totally unable to cope with all of this! I'm sure that I have lost my only grandchildren to their new grandparents and I very much doubt that I will ever be able to

find room in my heart for all of my new step-grandchildren. But I've promised myself that I will try.

I often think of those happy years when we all lived as neighbors on our friendly street. Do remember me to the folks I knew. How I would love to come back to see you all. Someday I plan to do just that.

As ever, yours,
Julie.

In this age of serial relationships, short-time marriages, and divorces and remarriages, the role of step-grandparent is one in which many of us find ourselves involved. The reality of this becomes apparent when we learn that one out of every four marriages ends in divorce and that 80 percent of all divorced persons remarry. We grandparents are caught in the middle. Our children may change their mates, but our ties to our grandchildren cannot be so easily broken. We remain their biological grandparents forever, so of course we feel deprived and fearful when our grandchildren must be shared with new grandparents.

I can understand Julie's despair. It is a tragedy to lose contact and communication with our grandchildren or to have their relations with us become diluted and distant. I wonder, though, if Julie isn't being too negative and is closing her mind to some possible options of continuing to share in the lives of her grandchildren. If daughters-in-law have experienced real understanding and acceptance from their mothers- and fathers-in-law, they frequently value this relationship and choose to continue it even when their marriages are broken. They make opportunities for the children to keep in touch with their grandparents through visits, letters, and gifts. The children, too, form a natural link between biological and step-grandparents, and meaningful relationships are often formed between these two sets of grandparents with the children as their common bond. I am sure that children who live in such a permissive, somewhat impersonal society as ours need to love and be loved by many warm, caring adults, in addition to their parents. Holidays and birthdays, as well as vacation visits, give us welcomed occasions to reach out to our grandchildren with the assurance of our continuing love and concern. Whether the grandchildren and the new step-parent accept such overtures will depend on their own maturity as well as their sensitivity to our feelings and needs.

A DECALOGUE FOR GRANDPARENTS

Recently a group of grandparents, concerned over the many pressures that they saw within the family life of their children, met for a series of discussions on how they, as third-generation family members, could maintain closer intergenerational communication and relationships. As the program ended they wrote the following DECALOGUE FOR GRANDPARENTS. They agreed that anyone who could live up to all of these expectations would be a paragon of virtue, but it was worth giving them a try.

A DECALOGUE FOR GRANDPARENTS

1. I will try to remember as I grow older that I will probably need my children and grandchildren more than they will need me.
2. I will try not to control the lives of my children but respect and trust them, leaving them free to grow into their own world, one that didn't exist when I was young.
3. I will try not to feel guilty if I am critical of things that my children and grandchildren do and say. My love for them does not commit me to approve or disapprove of their actions.
4. I will try not to be so indulgent with my grandchildren that I make it difficult for their parents, nor will I ever knowingly come between them and their parents.
5. I will try not to feel hurt when I am not thanked for gifts, or self-pity when they are thoughtless of me.
6. Remembering that each generation must make its own mistakes, I will try not to preach or insist on my way of doing things. I will keep myself available as a source of advice and assistance should I be asked.

Figure 5. What we continue to have in common with our children will be more important than anything that may seem to divide us.

7. In order that old age will hold a minimum of negative overtones for my children and grandchildren, I will try to maintain my physical and emotional health and remain a vital, attractive person.
8. If I should become unable to care for myself, I will try to accept my increasing dependency with grace and trust, cooperating to the degree that I am able in making the necessary decisions for my care.
9. Although I may feel closer to some of my children and grandchildren than to others, I will not knowingly create situations that will cause jealousy and friction among them.
10. In order not to create conflict and hurt feelings among my children and grandchildren I will make a will so that my estate will be distributed according to my wishes. Also, I will leave instructions for the distribution of my personal possessions so that each of my grandchildren may have some favorite object that I have personally designated for him or her.

Conclusions

In the years ahead, changes may continue to make the social and emotional distances between us and the younger generation family members even wider, as broken marriages and single parent families increase and new life-styles and marriages across ethnic and racial lines become more common and acceptable. What we will continue to have in common with our children through the years, however, will be much more important than anything that may seem to divide us. Our lives will remain inextricably and profoundly bound to theirs. Our concern for their welfare and pride in their accomplishments and careers will continue to be one of our major life interests, their continuing love and affection one of our deepest needs.

Chapter 6

LONELINESS — WE ALL EXPERIENCE IT

People are lonely
because they build walls
instead of bridges.
JOSEPH FORT NEWTON

"ALL older people are lonely." That is what 60 percent of the younger people queried in a recent survey by Louis Harris Associates believe. However, only 12 percent of older adults agree, according to the report. That all older people are lonely is one of the many myths held so widely in our society. We older ones readily acknowledge that we do feel lonely many times and under certain circumstances. But this is not a new experience! We have felt lonely at many other times in our lives. There was the very first day at school when we had to make it with a new teacher without the protection of our mothers; our first party as an adolescent when no one asked us to dance; and that first Christmas after we were married and living too far from home to celebrate it with our families.

We have known, too, an existential kind of loneliness that accompanied peak experiences in our lives when the beauty of a scene or the quality of a human encounter became so overwhelming that we were lost within it. I remember so well this kind of loneliness when I was travelling in Switzerland several years ago. I had left the tour group to make a side trip on my own to Zermatt to get a close-up view of the Matterhorn. The little cog train bound for Zermatt was filled with Swiss families and groups of happy tourists, all on their way to the picturesque village for the celebration of St. Mary's Day. Suddenly, I felt desperately alone and lonely. As the train stopped and the passengers began to pour out, I found myself confronted by two Catholic sisters coming out of the forward coach to the common exit. Instinctively I stepped back and let them precede me onto the platform. I, in turn, followed after, and as I stepped down, there they were, one on either side of the steep step, reaching out to hold my hand and steady my step as I alighted. It was more than a friendly gesture. There were no words spoken, only smiles and my hands pressed by theirs for ever so short a time. Soon we were on our separate ways never to meet again. But their message to me had come through without their spoken word, which I could not have understood. "Welcome to our country, we are glad to share its beauty with you, and may St. Mary bless you." That night, in the last long thoughts before sleep, there came over me an overwhelming sense of finiteness and aloneness, of being a little speck of humanity set down for the night on the steep slopes of the Alps, overshadowed by the mighty and awesome Matterhorn.

No, loneliness is not a new experience for us; it is part of being human, of knowing that we are inextricably involved with others and at the same time irrevocably alone. In old age loneliness seems to become accelerated. It is part of the loss and desolation that inevitably follows the physical and emotional separation we experience when one's spouse dies, as adult children become submerged in their own interests and the stresses and demands of their own families, and as the number of one's close friends dwindles. We begin to sense a lack of connectedness to primary persons, and isolation and loneliness move in to fill the void. Many of us feel distinct limitations to replace the losses that have triggered our loneliness and only reluctantly realize that if no new relationships are made, the loneliness remains.

REFLECTIONS ON

LONELINESS AS A CHARACTERISTIC OF OUR SOCIETY

Far-reaching changes in our society seem to heighten the loneliness of young and old alike. So many forces today are pulling people apart. Relationships at so many critical intersections of our lives, in marriage, the family, between generations, and in the church, have become lost or greatly weakened. Our cities have become so big, blighted, and impersonal, and the violence all about alerts us to be cautious in relating to strangers. We seem to have lost our experience of community and neighborliness. We too readily withdraw into the security of our homes, and our enforced aloneness accentuates our loneliness. We soon feel alienated and cut off from others. Our next door neighbors remain strangers, and we rarely talk to our seatmates on buses or smile at the persons next in line at the supermarket. We treat persons as objects and play psychological games which may, for a brief time, give us the illusion that we are cared about. We identify with the heroine or hero of the soap opera on television and listen to radio talk shows when the voice becomes for us the person. We join lonely hearts clubs whose ads fill our newspapers. We give and receive the Kiss of Peace in our churches in a momentary encounter of intimacy, often with perfect strangers. We embrace, in encounter and therapy groups, individuals whom we have never seen before and may not ever again. "Have a nice day" has become an almost perfunctory greeting from the gas station attendant, checker at the supermarket, and teller at the bank. Such contrived expressions of intimacy may temporarily relieve our feelings of loneliness, but they provide no real or permanent solution for our days of unpeopled aloneness.

Holidays and anniversaries are often times of intense loneliness. In other years these were the times when we, with more certainty, knew the joy and zest of living and the deep emotional security of belonging and being loved. Now as holidays approach, if we are alone, feelings of self-pity and a kind of personal shame seem to take over. We try to retreat from the hurt of our memories and what we interpret as the pity of others by running away, if we can afford it, on face-saving trips and cruises. Thus we try to escape into the less emotionally charged world of strangers. Our loneliness is not filled; for a short time it may be forgotten.

Feelings of nostalgia and loneliness often pervade our holidays even when our spouses are still living and we celebrate with our children and grandchildren. "I don't know when I have felt so lonely," one of my friends confided to me after she and her husband returned from a long anticipated trip to spend Christmas with their daughter, son-in-law, and grandchildren. "The children were so thoughtful and hospitable and did everything they could to make us feel welcome and have a good time. Groups of their friends were in and out all during the holidays, and several families with whom they share other occasions joined us for Christmas dinner. They, in turn, invited us to their homes, and we really had a beautiful time. It wasn't until we returned home that Bill and I were both able to talk about how lonely and empty we had felt during our visit."

When we celebrate holidays and anniversaries with our children and their families, we must be ready to accept the fact that many of the homey practices and family rituals in which we have invested so much meaning over the years may no longer have a place in the celebration as it is practiced by our children. They have been replaced by unfamiliar and, sometimes for us, uncomfortable new patterns. Their friends, strangers to us, share their attention and hospitality; our grandchildren, too, are busy with their friends and interests; even the menu for the holiday feast may be different: the creamed onions and minced meat pies may be missing! The nostalgia which seems to submerge us is inevitable. It can be no other way! Our rituals and meanings around holidays are uniquely ours; our children and grandchildren are in the process of developing their own. They may choose to include ours, but the decision is theirs.

We will soon learn that we cannot solve our loneliness by playing games of being brave. Loneliness can only be handled if we accept that it is real and that we, and we alone, have the responsibility of dealing with it. Others may reach out in many caring ways to encourage and support us, but its solution is ours. Caring must begin with us. Then it can move outward and join us again to others. If we can learn not to be frightened by our loneliness but accept and deal with it, some of the void will be filled with a new sense of strength and self-mastery. From it will emerge a deeper understanding and compassion for other people. If, on the other hand, we become victims of loneliness, we will soon find ourselves totally absorbed in self-pity and despair.

Some Reflections on

Loneliness and Maslow

I recently reread *Toward a Psychology of Being* by Abraham Maslow, a contemporary psychiatrist. Maslow believes that we develop our highest potentials as human beings only when certain social and emotional needs are met. He lists these as our need for health and safety, belonging and affection, respect and self-respect, self-actualization, and significance. Not one of these basic needs for achieving wholeness can be met by a robot, calculator, or computer. They can only be met through our relationships with other human beings whose lives and love confirm us. Maslow points out that it is essential for our continuing mental health to make new relationships to replace those that are lost by death or other reasons, but these new relationships may have a different quality from those we made in early life periods that gave so much meaning to our lives. To make new and intimate friends when one is old is not easy. Much depends on our health, where and how we live, whether we are physically able to move about freely in the community, and whether we really care enough to make the effort. We have no choice! Living without the stimulation of close contact with caring people will only increase our loneliness and depression and accelerate degenerative changes in our minds and bodies.

SOME LONELY PEOPLE I HAVE KNOWN

How well we cope with loneliness in our older years will, of course, depend on how successful we were in dealing with it in earlier periods of our lives. How others have met their loneliness, sometimes successfully and sometimes unsuccessfully, may help us to understand and cope with our own. Mrs. B., Phyllis G., and Fred are three very lonely people. They are all handling loneliness in their own characteristic ways.

Mrs. B. is a well-educated, intelligent neighbor of mine, whose husband was never able to provide all of the luxuries and the social and cultural opportunities she longed for. This, coupled with the fact that she never had children, made her see herself as a deeply deprived person. A niece and her family who live in the same community are now her only living relatives. They are extremely attentive and thoughtful of her, visit frequently, and include her in all family and holiday celebrations, as well as occasional vacation trips. She is surrounded by more thoughtful, caring friends than any other older person I know. They take her shopping, to concerts, and to the theater, bring her flowers and homemade treats. Often I have found myself wistfully wishing that I, too, had as many good friends. Nothing, however, that her niece or her friends do for her seems to be enough. She complains to all who will listen, "Everyone has forgotten me. No one loves me. All I have to look forward to is death." She has such an insatiable need for love and attention that she continually manipulates her niece and all of her friends in a frantic attempt to completely absorb them for her own. She seems totally unable to initiate any effective solution for her own emptiness. By her pleas of helplessness and self-pity she tries to place the burden of her loneliness on others. Her friends are all beginning to realize that Mrs. B.'s needs are so limitless that they can never meet them, no matter how loving and caring they are.

In trying to help her, her friends now find themselves the victims of Mrs. B.'s complaints and unrealistic demands. She is fast becoming a manipulative old woman from whom her friends now try to escape. They acknowledge that they can no longer cope with the frustrations and their increasing guilt in not being able to measure up to her demands and expectations. Mrs. B. will probably never be able to handle her loneliness which now threatens to destroy her until she experiences again the joy and pain of loving another person more than she loves herself.

I've thought so often of Phyllis G. since I met her the other day in the dress department of one of our large stores. I noticed her casually going through the racks. When she caught sight of me she seemed to try to hide so she wouldn't have to speak. I had recently read of her husband's death, and my impulse was to reach out to her to express my sympathy. I've known Phyllis for over fifty years, ever since we both used to make cakes for the bake sales at our woman's club. I remember still how she always apologized for her cakes, even though they were every bit as good as any of the others. In fact, she always seemed to depreciate herself and everything she did or had. She rarely spoke up in the club meetings and always refused to serve on a committee or be an officer. "Oh, no," she would explain, "I would never be able to take that responsibility." She always kept on the fringes of the group. I soon began to sense that Phyllis did not feel too O.K. about herself. I wondered if she had been made to feel that way early in childhood, perhaps unwittingly, by her parents or older siblings. Her husband, Frank, must have been a very supportive and understanding man who had been able to help her accept herself as a good wife and mother.

I had rarely seen Phyllis since our woman's club days. As I saw her again I sensed her loneliness. After some initial small talk I suggested that we go to a nearby tearoom for a visit. There she was able to tell me about Frank's death, her infrequent visits with her children who lived in the East, and how alone she now felt. She came downtown every afternoon and spent the time going in and out of the stores. She confessed that she rarely bought anything, but she could pass the time and be among people without having to relate to them. All of my suggestions of how she could meet congenial age-mates were met with the same response: "Thank you for your concern, but I'm really not interested in meeting people. I never feel comfortable, and it's too late now to try."

I wish I had felt that I could say to Phyllis what I know to be true. Rarely do people purposely hurt or reject us. It is only our own "I'm not O.K." feelings that interpret what other people say and do as rejection. Phyllis is like so many other women and men who have gone through life holding on to such negative feelings about their own worth. When they lose those who have accepted them and made them feel all right, they find it very difficult to reach out again to others, especially to those of the opposite sex. Women like Phillis are often not flexible enough to make relationships with new persons and find satisfactions and values in new experiences. They feel that they may be misunderstood, even laughed at, and rejected. For them the risk is so great that they settle for impersonal casual contacts. Their loneliness mounts and soon permeates their entire lives. Although it is hard for many women to admit their feelings to others, their loneliness will become manageable only when they can accept themselves as persons worthy of love.

As I drove home after my encounter with Phyllis, I thought about other friends who had recently lost life-mates and were experiencing deep loneliness. I thought of Fred. Many of us had frequently invited Fred to come for dinner after Helene's death, hoping that we could help fill his loneliness. When it was time to go home he would invariably say, "Now don't you folks worry about me. I never get lonely." We all knew what a cop-out this was. He and Helene had had a very happy marriage and close relationship. Denying his loneliness seemed to be the only way he had found to cope with it. He simply could not tolerate having others feel sorry for him. He held tenaciously to his self-image as a totally self-reliant man. To be otherwise would, he thought, show weakness.

OBSERVATIONS ON

HOW MEN HANDLE LONELINESS

The ways in which men handle their deep emotional feelings of loneliness differ in marked ways from women. In our society it is easier for women to make friends with other women than for men to establish meaningful ongoing relationships with other men. Women keep in touch with one another through telephone visits and lunching together; they meet to play bridge, to shop, and to go on trips. Also, they are more apt to retain close affectional ties with siblings and kin. Men often try to escape their loneliness by accelerating the pace of their daily activities. Their constant merry-go-round busyness gives them and all who are concerned about them the illusion that all is well with them. This becomes for most men only a desperate self-destroying facade. Having been robbed of their feelings of self-worth when jobs terminated, and feeling abandoned and hopelessly alone when their spouses died, many men seem to be totally unable to cope. They often seek to anesthetize themselves with alcohol, drugs, and tranquillizers or choose suicide as a way out. Studies show that there are proportionately more suicides among men seventy-five and older than for any age group. On the other hand, many men when they are widowed move quickly to reestablish old friendships and make new ones, which develop into satisfying social patterns, and many times remarry. Among those men and women whose spouses have been dead for five or more years, there seem to be fewer complaints of loneliness.

There are some men in our society who seem to experience minimum loneliness in old age. They are known as "loners." They are individuals who early in life cut all ties with their families and roamed around the country and the world. They never married, drifting from job to job, and never seemed to develop the ability or desire to make close relationships. In old age they do not seem to experience the isolation and loneliness that a diminishing circle of primary persons brings to other men. In old age they appear not to miss what they have never had.

For most of us, however, loneliness after the loss of loved persons is inevitable, and the only lasting solution for it is to win for ourselves again the attention and intimacy of other persons. Many men and women find that joining senior centers, living in residential settings with other older adults, and attending adult education classes and joining others on tours provide easy and nonthreatening ways to make meaningful new relationships.

OBSERVATIONS ON

LONELINESS AND THE SINGLE WOMAN

A headline in a news story caught my attention recently.

"Are Single Seniors Less Lonely?" it queried. The article reviewed a recent study of older women who had never married. It was carried on in Marquette University in Milwaukee, Wisconsin. The research findings indicated that single older women as a group seem to be relatively free from chronic loneliness. Such women, the research reports, constitute a distinct type of social personality. Without the problems and responsibilities around child rearing and family living, their lives had been far less complicated and stressful than those women who had married. The single woman had to learn to handle her own problems and make sound decisions and judgments. She could never lean on another or depend on someone else to create her happiness for her. She had faced the necessity to develop her inner resources and cope with her instinctual drives and tensions around her sexuality as an emotionally healthy individual outside of marriage. Such women in old age, according to the study, are more likely to be well integrated and more content than either the older widow or divorced woman. On the other hand, the study revealed, the older woman who would have chosen marriage but did not attain it often in old age shows a bitterness and brittleness that drives others from her.

What a change we have seen in the social attitudes around the roles and status of the single older woman in our society. Fifty years ago the unmarried daughter rarely worked outside her home. She became the caretaker of her parents as they aged and the "Aunty" to her nieces and nephews and other people's children. Many retired professional women who are our age mates broke from that restrictive pattern when they were young. Their attitudes and their insistence on the freedom to live their own lives made them the "women libbers" of their day. Since, in their youth, marriage and careers were considered by most women to be mutually exclusive, they chose to remain single and have professional careers.

For older women, whether never married, widowed, or divorced, the threat of loneliness if they do not choose to marry or remarry can often be met by carefully planned living arrangements. Society no longer frowns on a woman living alone or with one or more women or with a man. However, the curiosity about lesbianism, homosexuality, or living with a man outside of marriage makes many sensitive women hesitate to do so. They fear such personal accusations even when the relationship is entirely platonic. Shared living arrangements have many advantages. Two or more incomes make possible a more spacious and comfortable home, as well as a higher standard of living and congenial companionship, intellectual stimulation, and a fuller social life. Shared living arrangements also assure emotional support for each member of the household and someone to fill dependency needs during illness. The success of such living arrangements as a solution to loneliness depends on the willingness of those involved to grant to the others as much privacy and autonomy as each requires and desires.

SOME REFLECTIONS ON

ALONENESS AND LONELINESS

We often confuse loneliness and aloneness. The loneliness that encompasses us when we lose a loved person forces us into more aloneness, but solitude or aloneness is not necessarily a negative experience. Many individuals who have a strong sense of self-esteem really enjoy being with themselves. A certain amount of solitude is essential for one's emotional well-being. It makes possible the opportunity to reflect, evaluate, and integrate into our thinking and feelings our day-by-day experiences. We see new perspectives and are able to accept much that formerly troubled us and seemed so important. We no longer feel such an overriding pressure to please others. We take time to pace and face ourselves, to feel our own hurts, to know our own joys, to rejoice over what has been and look forward to what may yet be. We learn anew to feel compassion for others and even for ourselves.

I can still feel the apprehension and anxiety that filled me when I realized, as my seventieth birthday approached, that I would be spending it alone. My friend with whom I share a home and so many of the graces and joys of daily life had suddenly been called East by a family emergency. Since it was summer and other close friends were on vacation trips, and there were no members of my family who lived near enough to celebrate with me, I faced the fact that I would be alone. One's seventieth, I thought to myself, was some kind of a milestone, but there would be no one to affirm it so for me! I accepted that I had several choices of what I could do and feel that day. I could retreat into self-pity and loneliness, or I could spend the day in self-discovery and a celebration of my own life. With an unmistaken sense of excitement the decision was quickly made. I would spend the day at the beach, a place that I loved above all others. Here I always felt totally alive and whole. I would spend the hours walking along the shore, have my lunch and rest in the warm sunshine, and give myself uncluttered time to feel, wonder at, and be thankful for life and for my own seventy years of it.

My gifts that day were different from those of other years: The momentary company of a three-year-old who looked up suddenly from building his sand castles to say "Hi" and then trusted me enough to accept one of my cookies; the bevy of sandpipers that came within inches of me as they skittered along the receding waves to snatch up the tiny marine animals that had been left on the sand; the delight at watching a fast game of frisbee between two lanky adolescent boys; the rolling swells as they pounded on the beach with the incoming tide and deposited at my feet countless smoothly polished stones; finally there was the hot July sun as it began to set into the horizon, marking unmistakenly the end of my special day. Suddenly a deep down-to-the-bone tiredness seemed to catch up with me, and I was ready to return home. As I went early to bed with a favorite book that night, I found myself filled with a special kind of joy and zest, thankful for the gifts and the flavor of this particular birthday, my seventieth.

Each day I grow more aware that there are times in our lives in which our longing and emptiness cannot be filled by others no matter how close and dear they are to us. This is a longing that has strong overtones of yearning to be caught up by and related to whatever gives ultimate meaning to all of life. In these days when scientists and mystics have led us far out into the unlimited spaces of the universe and down into the deep places of our own psyches, this existential loneliness becomes more profound. It is difficult to feel at home and at ease in a universe that has become increasingly vast. In the far reaches of our minds and spirits we try to comprehend that the energy that keeps the planets on their courses moves also within us, binding us to one another and to the universe itself. Nothing, we learn, is finished. All, including man, is in the process of becoming. We sense that this loneliness is not related to any outer circumstances of our lives. It is a part of the human condition, a part of the reality and destiny of us all. As we grow older, according to Carl Jung, we turn inward, seeking to discover within our own center the meaning of our lives and that of all life in general. This inward journey becomes for us a fulfilling and integrating quest. It is a journey on which no one walks with us. We have "to walk it by ourselves."

Chapter 7

KEEPING ALIVE WHILE WE LIVE

We are fully ourselves only in relation to each other.
The *I* detached from a *Thou* disintegrates.
I do not find you by chance,
I find you by an active life of reaching out.
Rather than passively letting things happen to me,
I can act intentionally to make them happen.
I must begin with myself, true,
But I must not end with myself —
The truth begins with two.

ANONYMOUS

UNLESS they are loved, newborn babies cannot live. Providing the essential cuddling and stroking for each of the Rohrer quintuplets, born recently in Baltimore, called for some special planning by their doctor. He ordered the infants removed each hour from their individual isolettes and assigned a team of nurses to help their young mother hold and fondle each baby. Without this, the doctor said, they would not have lived. The hunger for physical and emotional security of being close to and touched by another human being is present at the moment of birth. We feel this need throughout our lives. It persists until death.

As shown in the preceding chapter on loneliness, we have become aware that it will be essential for us to continue to keep ourselves intimately involved with other people if we are to find zest and meaning for our days. Our ability to do this will depend in large part on how we feel about ourselves. If we doubt our own worth, then we will tend to withdraw from others, become egocentric and full of self-pity. A retreat into illness and neurotic self-seclusion will follow. On the other hand, if we feel good about ourselves and our self-worth, our morale will remain high. After any crisis or period of grief, we often need a "rest stop" to sort out our thoughts and take emotional soundings of our lives. When we have done this, and for some of us it takes longer than for others, we will be ready to re-engage in making new relationships and developing new interests. At such times many of us decide to shed former responsibilities and social involvements which may now seem extraneous, dull, and meaningless. We long to grow in new directions and make new friends who will share our new interests. We have an opportunity now to restructure our time and be as active or passive as our needs dictate. We can say yes or no to invitations and to the expectations that others put upon us. We no longer need to do anything just because we feel that we "ought."

REFLECTIONS ON

NEW PATTERNS FOR OUR OLDER ADULT YEARS

Because we enjoy working and need to supplement our retirement income, some of us start second and even third careers. We are helped to do this through a number of community-based employment programs for older workers. One of these, the Senior Community Service Employment Program, is sponsored by the American Association of Retired Persons and funded by the Older Americans Act. This program is now operating in more than ninety U. S. cities. Others of us join political action and consumer groups, become members of senior centers, and attend college and adult education classes. We welcome all new challenges and experiences! Soon we hear ourselves explaining, "I'm busier now than at any other time in my life!"

I often think of my friend Ruth who chose a totally new pattern for her interests and activities. Ruth's children and friends were unbelieving when she announced that she had just closed the deal on the purchase of a small home in a nearby rural community. The first break in old patterns had come for her when her husband Ned had died five years before. Now with her own retirement from a successful law practice, she

Figure 6. We are fully ourselves only in relation to each other.

faced the necessity to plan for the years ahead. "What in the world are you thinking of?" queried her friends when she announced her plans. "How do you expect to find congenial friends and stimulating activities in that small town?" She confidently explained that she wanted to live where she could easily walk wherever she needed to go, and that she would resist joining any social groups until she felt ready.

Ruth had always been a history buff with a real passion for English history. She confessed that she wanted above all to have time to pursue that interest. Her first letters to me were glowing in her delight in the university extension course in Elizabethan history that she was attending at the local high school. Soon came news of her plan to attend a seminar at Oxford University that summer. She said she wanted to study that period in English history that gave birth to the values and ideals that formed the basis of our own Declaration of Independence. The bicentennial year became for Ruth one of the most exciting of her entire life. On her Christmas greeting to me last year she wrote,

> I seem now to have gotten my life all together for the years ahead. My days are mine to use as I see fit. I decided when I moved here that if ever I was to do my own thing, this was my opportunity. It's not that I didn't have a satisfying and happy marriage, career, family, and social life. It's because I did that I now feel that I am free to enjoy something new and different. One of these days, I may just *do nothing* and not feel the least guilty. That may be the most fun of all! I have always considered that so wicked!

Keeping involved in activities and interests that are meaningful to us is beyond a doubt the best way to continue to feel good about ourselves. There are no activities that are off limits just because we have had a certain number of birthdays. Why shouldn't we, if these are our interests, swim and jog, go on picnics and travel, take yoga, dance, or sit in quiet meditation? Why can't we too wear funny clothes and go to some of our neighborhood's favorite hangouts, eat ice cream cones and pizzas, laugh and tell jokes, especially on ourselves. "The old should act their age," some will say. And so we would be if we were doing what we really enjoy! To continue to be completely ourselves in a society that is trying to level us down to conform with its ideas of what older people are like means to fight one of the hardest battles of our lives.

OPPORTUNITIES UNLIMITED FOR GROWING

Census figures reveal at the end of every decade that we older Americans comprise even larger percentages of the population. In the last ten years the number of persons aged seventy-five and over increased three times as fast as those from sixty-five to seventy-four. Community, governmental, educational, religious, and voluntary groups are now aware of their opportunities and responsibilities to develop programs and services to meet our interests and needs. Multipurpose senior centers, Lifetime Learning and Emeritus Colleges, Foster Grandparents, Retired Senior Volunteers, Grey Panthers, American Association of Retired Persons, CETA (Comprehensive Employment Training Act), and SCORE (Senior Corps of Retired Executives) are to be found in most of our communities. Information about these resources can be provided by the Hot Lines of community information and referral services and local offices of area agencies on aging. Essentially these programs provide unlimited opportunities for individuals to grow through continuing education, volunteer services, social action, and enriching social activities.

The importance of becoming involved in such programs has been substantiated in recent studies by Doctor Marjorie F. Lowenthal, Professor of Social Psychology at the University of California in San Francisco. In studies of first admissions to mental hospitals, she found that 31 percent of the patients had no social involvement either with relatives, friends, or community groups. As social involvements increased, the percentage who became mentally ill decreased. Twenty-two percent of the group limited their involvement to close relatives; 11 percent also visited friends occasionally and attended social gatherings. The percentage of admissions dropped to 5 percent for individuals who were actively involved in social groups and community activities.

LIFE-TIME LEARNING

Unless we make an effort to keep our minds flexible and active and continue to update our knowledge, we will soon begin to feel unrelated to today's world. TV programs, as well as our daily papers, bombard us with facts, but we need dialogue and input from others in order to interpret and give these facts perspective and make them relevant to our own lives. How reassuring it is to learn from psychologists that as long as we maintain our health, our learning ability does not decline. It may take us a little longer than our grandchildren to learn new facts, but once learned, we use them with as much and sometimes greater facility than they do.

The ability of older people to maintain a high level of mental functioning is well documented in the lives and accomplishments of many men and women who have been our contemporaries. We think of Frank Lloyd Wright who was still actively designing unique and beautiful buildings when he died at age eighty-five. Doctor Lillian Martin, after she retired at eighty as a psychology professor at Stanford University, started in San Francisco the first counselling center in our country for older adults. Imogene Cunningham, a photographer, was awarded a prized Guggenheim fellowship on her eighty-seventh birthday. At ninety-two she began work on *After Ninety*, a collection of photographic portraits of old people, which was published just after her death at ninety-three. Cardinal Angelo Roncalli became Pope John XXIII at seventy-six. The great cellist, Pablo Casals, vibrant at ninety, was still teaching groups of young students and performing in concert. Leopold Stokowski at the age of ninety-four was still leading recording sessions of some of the great symphonic orchestras. Just before he died he had signed another four-year contract. You may say that these were all unusually gifted and creative people, and you would be right. But they give proof that creativity, sustained ability, and the power to enrich one's life, as well as that of the society and the culture, need not terminate in old age. Creativity in one's later years requires an abiding interest in life and a conviction that we can continue to grow, learn, and create to the very end of our days.

Encouraging, too, are the positive attitudes in most of our communities about the responsibility of public education to provide educational opportunities for us as well as for younger students. Many community colleges, universities, and other degree-giving institutions now have policies of open admission for students over sixty-two years of age. Some colleges have developed curriculum specifically for older students. These new colleges are called by a variety of names, such as Emeritus College, Lifetime Learning, Continuing Learning in Retirement, and Elder-Berry College. A group of twenty-eight community colleges in northern California have developed the Nor-Cal Learning Consortium to teach courses for older adults through newspaper articles and television programs. In New England an excellent program of Elder Hostels has been developed which arranges for older people to reside on college campuses and attend summer school. This plan is spreading to other parts of the country. To be on a college campus in wheelchairs, with white canes and hearing aids, to read in the library, eat lunch in the student lounge, and swing along the pathways to our classes with our younger classmates will bring learning experiences to young and old alike far beyond the pages of our textbooks.

The experiences of my friends Bill, Ellen, and Margaret illustrate the older person's desire and need for learning. Bill is eighty-eight years old. I was aware of his keen mind the first day he appeared in my class. He lingered one morning to share his feelings with such urgency and excitement, and the words came tumbling out. "I don't know why, whether I was too involved in my work, too worried over family problems, I don't know! I only know that I have been more open to new ideas in these last two years than at any time in my life. Now I've no time to lose. There is still so much I want to learn. I'm helping that blind girl, Eleanor. I read to her three afternoons each week. It's a great feeling helping the young . . ."

I am often asked what motivates an older person to want to

Figure 7. We can continue to grow, learn, and create to the end of our days.

continue to learn since he or she is not usually working toward a degree or a profession. Ellen explained her regular attendance at the Current Affairs lectures in these words: "I feel I have to keep up with what's going on in the world. I have college educated daughters and sons-in-law and a smart grandchild growing up. I just have to be an interesting person in my own right, not just 'Grandma.'" Then she added wistfully, "There's one thing that I really appreciate about Professor S. He treats me like an intelligent human being, instead of a child wanting to be entertained. I'm a college graduate and I'm challenged only by university-level education."

A recent letter from Margaret who moved away from the community soon after being in one of my classes certainly made my day. She wrote:

> *Dear Florence,*
>
> It is difficult for me now to realize that three years ago I came to your course, "The Older Adult Years — A Time To Be Real." I was at my wit's end then. At seventy-eight I found myself in a condition of mental numbness and physical tiredness. I thought the senility of old age had started! But in your class I met bright and alert age-mates. The information that you provided from the wide range of your experiences and studies gave evidence that getting older has its dangers but also its challenges and rewards. In digging out the cause of my listlessness I found I had relapsed into childhood, those years when we expect to be the center of attention, with someone else responsible to meet all our needs. When I became aware of what I was doing to really destroy myself, I decided it was time to change my thinking and my attitude. I live now with a new vitality and expect to continue for many more years. Let me tell you how this new purpose and energy carries me along, now that I am eighty-one.
>
> I am foremost so grateful that I was able to take care of my sick husband without outside help until he died. Now that he is gone, I have many hours to fill. I am active in the local Mental Health Association and serve on a committee interested in creating preventive mental health education for children and young people. In the Outdoor Art Club I participate in the Garden Section, the Literary Section, and the Conservation group. I attend courses in our local community

college and was happy when I was invited to become a member of its curriculum committee. Next semester the college will offer a class to help older adults realize that every decade of life has its own developmental crisis which brings many changes and demands new solutions. Finally, in the solitude of my home I am also writing an essay on what Freud has to say about old age. This is something I have always wanted to do. Enough for now, but I've been wanting to bring you up to date on what is happening to me.

Cordially yours,
Meg.

Not all of my friends share the same excitement and satisfaction as Bill, Ellen, and Margaret in keeping their minds and spirits alive and growing. Many daily lament, "There is nothing for me to do. I am too old to learn anything. I have no friends left, I'm so lonely and forgotten!" I find myself wondering what such people did in their youth. Did they enjoy only gossip sessions and bridge parties and talk mostly about the weather, their children, or business deals? When lonely men and women tell me, "I don't want to get involved," I can only hear what they are really saying, "I don't want to be disturbed in my little self-centered island." This is their choice, but where does it lead?

VOLUNTEER SERVICES

Albert Schweitzer, a gifted French organist, in answer to the queries of his friends as to why he gave up a brilliant musical career to go to Africa as a missionary doctor, replied, "You must give sometime to your fellowman. Do something for which you get no pay but the privilege of doing it. Remember, you don't live in this world alone. Your brothers and sisters are here, too." Many older adults agree with him. In a recent Louis Harris Poll, 2 million men and women past retirement age said they would welcome opportunities to serve as volunteers without pay.

In many communities we are being offered opportunities to volunteer our skills and knowledge, our love and caring, to day nurseries, handicapped and abused children, youngsters who have no grandparents nearby, recent newcomers to our country wanting to learn to read and write, troubled teenagers, single parents, the terminally ill and dying, and victimized and lonely older people. They all need us! And we need to be needed! Our volunteer jobs have, for many of us, a significance we did not always find in those for which we received payment. The plus is the significant role and meaningful contacts we have with caring individuals of all ages.

Tad E., who was formerly an insurance broker, operates a most successful telephone reassurance program for all shut-ins in the county from his wheelchair in a convalescent home. Jon, a ninety-four-year-old retired civil engineer, is called for once a week at a retirement home where he lives and is taken to a nearby elementary school where he tells the youngsters about engineering, shows them engineering drawings, and tells of some of his interesting experiences. "Captain Tim" is now an honorary member of a Boy Scout troop. His stories about his experiences as a licensed master aboard square riggers and his demonstrations of knot tying make him one of the most popular members of the troop. Molly D., who is now seventy-five-years-old, serves once a month at a hospital for the mentally ill, leading geriatric patients in exercises and games. Mrs. Kimble, who is herself a great grandmother, is a foster grandmother to children who are ill in the county hospital. "I have no patience at all with so many of my friends who spend all of their days playing bridge or watching soap operas on television when there are so many people who need help," she remarked to me. She has patience unlimited, however, as she plays with, comforts, and feeds the youngsters whom she proudly calls "my children."

A letter from my friend Lillian recently told me of the joy that she and her husband derive from their volunteer service with the Easter Seal Society's program for stroke victims. She wrote,

> *Dear Florence,*
>
> I've been wanting to write to tell you about what satisfaction Tom and I are finding in serving as volunteers in a wonderful program for men and women, young and old, who have had strokes. Being asked to serve in such capacity not

only surprised and made us slightly uncomfortable, it seemed about the most unlikely thing we could ever have thought of doing. Of what possible use could we be, a seventyish couple who had none of the seemingly necessary skills, no knowledge of speech or physical therapy, no special social skills, either.

Promising finally to look into it, we asked ourselves over and over, "What can we do?" not knowing that the real question was, "What can we be?" Can we be warm, caring, unstroke-damaged human beings, to meet socially once a week with stroke-damaged ones, exchanging concerns, playing word games, encouraging them to feel at ease, to talk and tease and laugh with us and with each other, to be genuinely excited and congratulatory over even the smallest speech difficulty overcome?

So you know what happened! The way that small group of people, some stricken at the peak of their middle age, some almost as old as we are, struggling with their various damaged bodies and brains to repair and relearn, is not only a beautiful, though humbling, experience, but food for the spirit.

Naturally, they are to us no longer a group of stroke victims. They are approximately one dozen gallant and courageous friends in whom we have a continuing interest and concern; friends who seem also, we hope, to care for us. I know you will be interested in the things that are making, in this very special way, our lives so full of meaning these days. I wish every one who feels so useless and lonely could have such a completely satisfying experience as Tom and I are having!

So many good wishes to you,
Lillian and Tom

There is for each of us, just as for Lillian and Tom, the right spot in our community, one that needs the skills and abilities and especially the warmth and wisdom that is ours. Volunteer bureaus and churches know the needs and can channel our services to those individuals and agencies who need us most.

SOCIAL ACTION

Senior Power — These words were boldly printed on oversized buttons worn by each member of a group of white-haired men and women I saw walking back and forth in front of the city hall. On inquiry I learned that they were demonstrating to show their discontent with the slow pace in which the housing program for older citizens was being developed. Their "power" could not be disputed in our community where individuals over sixty-five years of age constitute 17 percent of the voters. Amused smiles were obvious on the faces of many passersby as they viewed this determined group of older adults. Perhaps they were unbelieving that the pressure techniques formerly used only by youth in demonstrations, encounters, and sit-ins have become the modus operandi of their grandparents.

A recent dramatic example of our clout in national affairs was provided when the U. S. Senate spent weeks debating a drastic reorganization of the committee system of the federal government, which controls development of legislation from introduction of new bills to final passage. The original version of the reorganization bill abolished a number of important Senate committees, including the Committee on Aging. It is this committee that, for the past sixteen years, has effectively investigated issues relating to the elderly and paved the way for many important laws. National and local groups speaking for the elderly immediately began a grass roots campaign to save the Committee on Aging. Senators were bombarded by demands coming from us and our supporters all over the country. The results were decisive when the issue came to a vote on the floor of the Senate. The margin was overwhelmingly in favor. Ninety senators voted to save the committee with only four votes against. Here was a clear sign of "senior power" in the halls of Congress.

Young people concerned about human rights have become advocates for older people and work to give us support in bringing our problems and needs to the officials in the community. Many of us have not, in our younger years, been action-oriented. We are not now comfortable in the politics of confrontation and choose not to get involved in controversial issues. We excuse ourselves, saying, "I have fought my share of society's battles all my life. Now let younger people be responsible. I'm tired out." Is this a cop-out? Who has more time or is more able than we are to write our congressmen, send letters to the editors of our newspapers, and work actively for candidates and issues during political campaigns?

Who knows at first-hand better than we do what the current pressing problems are: high rents and property taxes, poorly operated and impersonal nursing homes, inadequate Social Security benefits, the high cost of medical care, crime, and the victimizing of older people. As governmental bureaucracies multiply and agencies concerned with our needs proliferate, we at times feel ourselves as pawns being moved about on political or community chess boards. As funds are appropriated in federal budgets and channeled down for the support of programs in local communities, we become acutely aware of the countless groups vying for funds to keep programs alive. We learn of new surveys and repeated studies to assess the needs of older Americans. We ask ourselves why more recognition and voice is not given to those of us who live intimately with these needs, and why we aren't asked to join with planners to shape our own destinies. We join such groups as the Grey Panthers, the American Association of Retired Persons, the Council of Older Americans, and Action Groups in Senior Centers, as these groups courageously and effectively give voice to our mounting needs and frustrations.

The problems that face older people in America today are far too vast for us to solve alone. Our efforts, however, can alert the total community. Our efforts, great or small, can be added to those of all others who are concerned about making our society one in which all people, including older people, really matter.

REFLECTIONS ON

THE YEARS WHEN WE CAN NO LONGER BE ACTIVE

Wouldn't it be wonderful if those additional years that medical science is working so hard to add to the human life span could be tacked right on to our productive middle years! Prolonging the frailer years of old age (gerontologists define these years as those after seventy-five) is thought by many to be a questionable goal. These are the years in which many of us begin to experience decreased energy and increased physical limitations. Many of us become increasingly unwilling to make the effort necessary to keep ourselves involved with people and activities that have kept our lives meaningful. Arthritis and broken hips may force us into inactivity; hearing losses, glaucoma, and cataracts cut some of us off from the people and activities we formerly enjoyed; heart attacks, strokes, and other debilitating conditions attack our bodies and many times require radical changes in life-styles. Now we must learn to accept a growing dependency on our mental and spiritual vigor rather than our physical strength.

A re-engagement in activities, at whatever level our physical limitations now may necessitate, will be less devastating for us if during earlier years we have developed a diversified range of interest and skills. We all know individuals like Professor S. and my friend Pearl, whose physical losses forced them to accept the fact that doors had closed. They had to find new ones to open. Professor S. had for many years taught English literature in our local high school. He had always been an avid reader and had a library that was the envy of us all. Recently a stroke and progressive glaucoma with a prognosis of blindness within the year caused all of his friends to wonder, How will Charlie ever cope? But cope he did! The last time I dropped in for a visit, I found him still "reading" through Talking Books which were sent to him from the state library. He was looking forward to the weekly visit from a high school student who came to read to him and bring him up to date on the latest school gossip.

Then there is Pearl. A fall had broken her hip and shattered her wrist. She was now able to be about using a walker, but the wrist, according to the doctor, had been so seriously injured that she probably would never have the full use of it. What a blow for Pearl! She is one of those grandmothers whose greatest joy in life has been crocheting baby blankets, knitting ski sweaters and socks, and piecing quilts for each of her grandchildren. "My biggest project is ahead," she often confided to her friends. "I have a dozen rosewood chairs in my attic that belonged to my grandmother. When I'm really an old lady I am going to needle point seats for them. Then each of my six grandchildren will have an heirloom that belonged to their great-great-grandmother." Pearl had completed just one when the accident occurred. What to do now? It would have been so easy to give up. Pearl's friends really feared that she would, but one day she announced to her daughter that she had enrolled in a painting class. "After all, I still have one good hand," she explained. Pearl never became a Grandma Moses, but her attempts at painting provided another outlet for a creativity that had given her so much pleasure throughout all of her life.

As I enjoy a large modern impressionistic painting of three birch trees that hangs on my living room wall, vibrant with bright oranges, yellows, blues, and greens, I think of my friend Edie, who is now ninety. Her studio is her small room in a retirement home in a beautiful valley setting. "I always paint sitting on the floor," she explains. "I need my bed and chairs to hold my paints and canvasses." This summer Edie flew back to Boston to attend a celebration at an art academy where she had studied in 1906. "I wouldn't have missed it," she told me. "You see, one of my latest paintings was chosen to be hung in the celebration show." Then almost wistfully she added, "After my surgery last year it was tough to get into painting again, really grim and slow. A change from oils to acrylics helped. And age has its points. There's more independence, better judgment, less need for approval, and an increased capacity for enjoyment and the exhilaration that painting brings." Edie, without a doubt, is back into painting again. Last week I went to a stunning one-woman show with over forty of her modern, exciting, colorful paintings, done within the past two years.

Experiences that leave us physically handicapped cause some of us to give up on life and decide that it is enough just to stay alive and be fed and cared for by others. This kind of petering out seems like such a tragic way to end our long adventure. If we are able to make the transition from the deprivations that our own personal tragedies have brought and accept re-

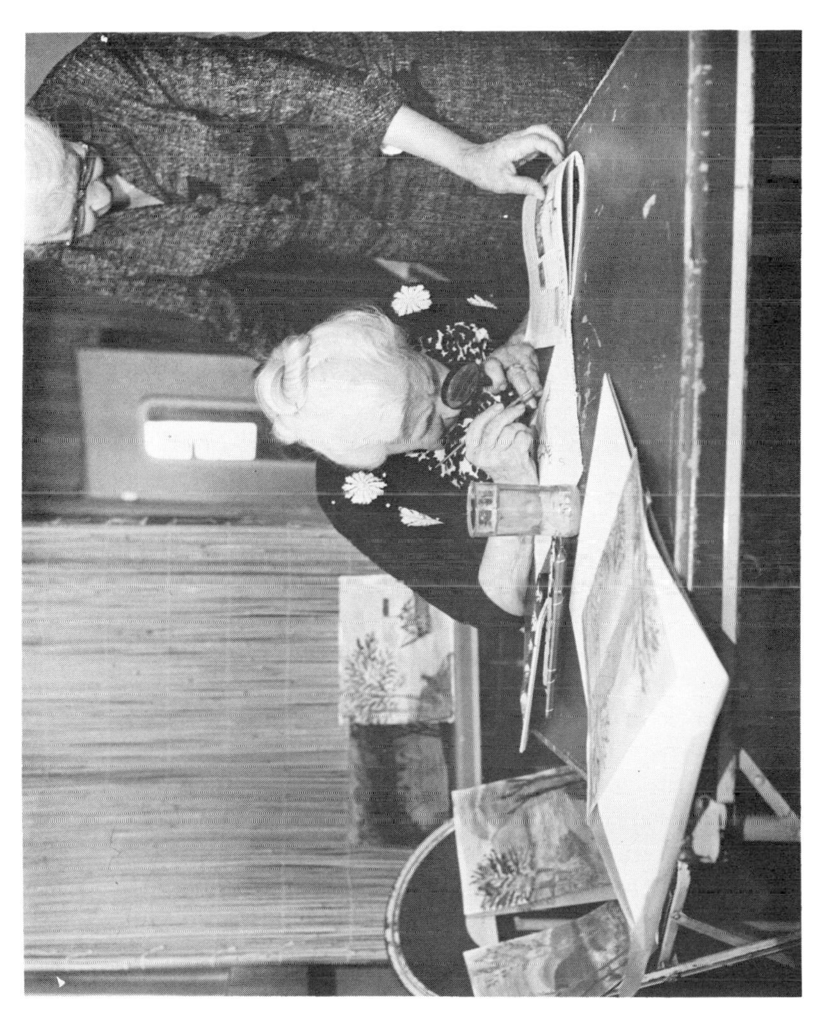

Figure 8. Physical handicaps need not stop learning.

engagement of our minds and spirits and what physical functioning is still ours, then the inner glow of our vibrancy and integrity may remain. We will find then that we will continue to have the support and love of caring persons. From them we will learn that continuing to exist in the thoughts and affections of even a few people is a very concrete and satisfying level of involvement up to the very end of life.

Chapter 8

HELPING OURSELVES TO HEALTH AND WELL-BEING

> Energy may be directed to any portion of the body, and if you do not block its action by disbeliefs, that portion will be cured.
>
> *The Nature of Personal Reality*
> BY JANE ROBERTS*

"IT'S just old age. You can begin to expect these aches and pains. You'll just have to live with them!"

Have you had a doctor or a friend tell you that lately? The myth that illness is a part of growing old is one that too many of us have too readily accepted and unconsciously programmed ourselves to fulfill. But it is not necessarily so! We all know individuals, and hopefully we are one of them, who maintain a high level of well-being and remain vibrant and active to the last days of their lives.

Have you ever awakened during the night with a nagging pain and thought, "Well this is it! Something is seriously wrong with me"? Most of us have! After days of worry and depression, fearing the worst, we finally muster courage to see a doctor. We then become one of 70 percent of all patients who consult doctors when no organic basis exists for their complaints. Many illnesses, we learn, are not caused by disease, germs, virus, or poison, but by emotional stress. We are more than our physical bodies whose parts sometimes get out of order. We have feelings, too! Each of us is a whole being with an interrelated and interdependent physical body, mind, and spirit. When each of these is functioning in harmony with the others, we feel at ease and well. If one is out of balance, we feel at dis-ease. A doctor can prescribe drugs and diet to alleviate the

---

*From the book, *The Nature of Personal Reality,* by Jane Roberts. ©1974 by Jane Roberts. Published by Prentice-Hall, Inc., Englewood Cliffs, New Jersey.

pain caused by a gastric ulcer, but the ulcer may well be in a person who is experiencing fears and frustrations. The ulcer cannot really be cured until the condition or the way in which one responds to the condition that has caused the stress and anxiety is changed.

HOLISTIC HEALTH, A MODERN CONCEPT OF HEALTH CARE

Today the skills of psychiatrists, psychotherapists, health educators, and spiritual teachers are all recognized as essential in working as partners with us and our doctors, surgeons, and nurses to deal with our illnesses and return to wellness. This holistic approach to well-being, of which we are daily becoming more aware, is an exciting new frontier of health care. It emphasizes the health of the whole person and the responsibility of each of us for one's own self-care.

Holistic health practitioners in no way take the position that doctors and their highly sophisticated diagnostic and treatment methods are not essential. It would be foolish to try to outguess our doctors when serious complaints develop, for they are the experts in the physical manifestations of illness. If we have not learned throughout our lives to handle the stresses that the body suffers, it is probable as we grow older that the accumulated scars left by stress and accidents will develop into one or more chronic conditions. Multiphasic examinations, including check-ups on blood pressure and blood sugar, chest X rays, pap smears, breast examinations, and glaucoma screening, require the services of the best medical technicians and doctors we can find. This is preventive medicine, and it makes sense.

High Energy Physics Brings New Understandings of the Nature of Our Physical Bodies

A whole new way of viewing man and the cosmos has developed since the days of Newton. He and the physicists of his time understood the universe and all objects within it as composed of solid, observable matter. They viewed the human body as a mechanism composed of many different parts and organs which, when they malfunctioned, had to be treated individually by drugs or surgery.

High energy physicists today view the universe and all matter, including our bodies, not as made up of many different parts but as many dynamic interrelated and interdependent energy fields. Depending on the frequency of its vibrations this energy manifests itself in matter, light, heat, and radiation. The findings of high energy physics have become the basis for the practice of holistic health care. The primordial energy which is the basis of the healing of our minds and bodies is the same as that manifest in the laws and order within the cosmos, in the rhythms seen in all nature, and in the interdependence of all living things. It is called by various names: God and the Supreme Being by religionists, Eternal Truth by metaphysicians, and Life Force by scientists.

It is difficult for many of us to think of our bodies as other than solid matter, confined within our own skins. We think of the bony framework, which gives the body form; of the muscles, which enable us to move in space; and finally, the various organ systems by which our lives are maintained! "But look further," say the physicists. "Your flesh, bones, and muscles that seem so solid are in reality made up of swiftly moving neutrons, protons, electrons, wave particles, and quarks. As they move at incredibly high rates of speed these subatomic particles discharge positive and negative energies."

Within the human body this exchange of energy takes place through three physiological processes: the blood which carries the oxygen and removes wastes from all the cells, the glands which secrete hormones that maintain the chemical balance of the body, and the brain and nervous system which carry all impulses and messages both within the body and from the outside environment. When we are emotionally "uptight" the blood vessels constrict and are limited in carrying out their essential functions. When we are anxious and under stress, metabolic and related endocrine changes take place, upsetting the chemical balance of the body. When energy is blocked in any of the systems and fails to circulate as it should, negative electrical charges then build up. If we are not able to discharge these in positive ways, the vital body systems do not receive as much positive energy as they need. As a result they slow down, and permanent organic changes may take place.

The brain and nervous system form a great switchboard for the energy flowing in and through our bodies. As the brain functions, it sets up its own energy patterns of rhythmic fluctuations called brain waves. In our day-to-day conscious activity, the energy patterns fall in beta waves; in meditation and relaxed states of the body, alpha waves predominate; and during sleep or deep relaxation, theta waves prevail. These waves are transferred from the brain through the nervous system and evoke direct responses from our cells. In a very real way then, we become what we believe and feel. Energy going out from our thinking creates the very condition we think about. Negative thoughts, such as "I'm tired," "I'm exhausted," or "I don't matter," are soon reflected in our facial expressions, in how we carry our bodies, and in our general appearance. We let our energy go into anti-life forces within and thus often victimize ourselves with our fears and destructive thoughts. It is as a wise teacher once said, "As a man thinks in his heart, so is he."

According to holistic health practitioners, controls can be learned and practiced on the negative energy that is activated by stress and anxiety. Conditions such as high blood pressure, heart disease, strokes, asthma, ulcers, and perhaps some forms of cancer are found to be stress related. Holistic health practitioners use techniques such as meditation, visualization, and relaxation — yoga, acupressure, and other autogenic exercises — to generate energy and focus it on the troubled areas of the body. Tensions are thus released and the chemical homeostasis of the body restored.

Opportunities to learn and practice these techniques are being offered in many communities in adult education classes, senior centers, mental health clinics, and meditation and holistic health centers. Through regular practice of such techniques we can learn to integrate our physical, emotional, and spiritual selves.

One program designed specifically for older adults is S.A.G.E., organized in 1974 in Berkeley, California, by Gay Luce, a psychotherapist. SAGE is an acronym for *S*enior *A*ctualization and *G*rowth *E*xperience. Working along with a therapist with extensive experience in body therapies and Gestalt psychology and a family counsellor, Gay Luce designed the SAGE program to use a number of different techniques to alter negative attitudes about aging. The methods used include music, massage, dance, deep breathing designed to revitalize the body and the mind, biofeedback, and creative art. A recent letter from my friend Eleanor was full and spilling over with enthusiasm about what the program is meaning to her.

Dear Florence,

You've always been so interested in what I am up to! I must bring you up to date. I have joined SAGE. It's proving to be one of the most exciting, rewarding, and life-expanding experiences I have ever had. After retirement from my Red Cross job I was totally happy for a time, and then I began to feel that I was missing out on life. I fear I had really settled for being an old lady. SAGE has changed all that. I've thrown away my negative attitudes about being seventy! Being a member of SAGE has put me in touch with so many new friends and experiences that have heightened my sense of self-worth and well-being. I have learned to be more relaxed by breathing properly, to experience my body through biofeedback, acupuncture, and acupressure; to feel the exhilaration and freedom of moving my body through yoga and Tai-Chi, and to be in my own inner center through meditation and music and art therapy. Somehow or other the whole world is my new world. It's new in the sense of energy, of producing, of meeting friends on a new level . . . I do honestly feel cosmic!

As you remember, I have always had high blood pressure, but I've learned to control it through autogenic exercise, which I do everyday. I was amazed and delighted when I discovered the other night that I could control indigestion and a very rapid heart beat with yoga. Best of all though, SAGE has really put me in touch with my whole self and increased the kinship I feel for people of all ages. You see, some of our teachers are bright young things who are so understanding and patient with us and so giving of themselves to us.

I wish every older person could have a SAGE experience. It really makes life begin at seventy!

I wanted to share my enthusiasm with you,

As ever,
Eleanor

HOLISTIC TECHNIQUES FOR SELF-CARE

Within the scope of this chapter we can look at only a few of the more popular nontraditional approaches to self-care and health maintenance as well as long established basic health practices. Workshops and classes in these may not be available in your community, but books listed in the bibliography will help you to help yourself.

Meditation

Recent studies of the brain show that it is divided into two hemispheres. Each has its different function, and each corresponds to two different and independent "minds." The left side of the brain is the seat of rational consciousness. It receives all the stimuli that come through our five senses from the outside world. It organizes and relates this information to that already stored in the brain and thus enables us to think and speak logically and rationally and to survive in the outer world.

The right side of the brain is the seat of creative consciousness. From here arise our intuitions, creativity and mental images, dreams, and visions. These make up our inner reality that transcends ordinary language and logical reasoning. Through meditation and other mind-altering techniques we are able to be in touch with and expand this inner reality.

Meditation for many people has been essentially a prayer form and devotional practice. The current interest in meditation is as a psychological experience. It is taught by psychotherapists, psychologists, holistic health practitioners, hypnotists, faith healers, and some clergy. There are many schools of meditation. Many of them, whose gurus have attracted large numbers of adherents in our country, are based on eastern mystical practices. Transcendental Meditation, or TM, as it is popularly called, is one of the largest and best known schools of meditation. It was introduced into this country in 1950 by Maharishi Mahesh Yogi and has won wide acceptance as a relaxation technique to heighten energy and inner consciousness. It is practiced by the old and young, professional men and women, athletes and politicians, in families, public schools, and prisons.

The meditation process consists of sitting quietly in a comfortable position with eyes closed and hands open with palms up or down on the thighs. By breathing deeply and directing the breath to various parts of the body, the meditator relaxes the various parts of the body. With each exhalation of his breath he tries to quiet all thinking processes by several means. The most familiar of such means is by paying attention to the breathing and the concentrated repetition of some word or phrase known as a mantra, or the concentration of the attention on some picture, flower, or symbol. With the conscious mind thus stilled, the body experiences complete relaxation. There are many ways to meditate; each person must explore and develop his own method. According to a recent poll, over six million Americans are practicing daily meditation in some form, from ten to thirty minutes once or twice daily.

Doctor Herbert Benson of Beth Israel Hospital in Boston has pioneered in the use of meditation as a technique for lowering blood pressure. In his recent book, *The Relaxation Response,* he reports that through the regular use of meditation his patients were able to lower their blood pressure 10 to 15 percent. The research of other doctors confirms his findings that the practice of relaxation will increase alpha waves and decrease oxygen consumption, heart rate, and blood pressure. Noticeable improvements in such psychosomatic complaints as tension headaches and insomnia were also noted. Patients began to think more clearly, feel calmer, solve problems more easily, and no longer needed daytime naps.

Visualization

Visualization or the use of imagery is also used in medita-

Figure 9. To be more relaxed and feel the exhilaration and freedom of moving our bodies.

tion. Because the visual cortex of the mind is large we can rather easily bring visual images into our consciousness. Visualization, therefore, is a powerful tool for activating and focusing energy on some physical condition or mental attitude which we wish to change. For example, if we are experiencing pain and discomfort or arthritis, we can then imagine specifically what it feels like and how much more comfortable we are when free of that pain. We can dwell on the picture of ourselves moving freely as happy, pain-free persons. This imaging focuses energy, causing it to flow to the painful areas, breaking down the tensions and bringing healing to them.

Such psychological support methods along with medical treatment are now being used with noticeable success in some special clinics for the control of cancer tumors. Doctors Carl and Stephanie Simonton report from their clinic in Fort Worth, Texas, that psychotherapeutic techniques have helped to control cancer in 80 percent of their critically ill patients. Although the relationship between emotional stress and the occurrence of cancer has not yet been scientifically analyzed, the Simontons theorize that when a person is under severe emotional strain, the energy from the body's immunity system is diverted to fight emotional and mental trauma. The natural ability of the body to fight disease is thus reduced, and the possibility that cells will become cancerous increases. At the Simonton clinic, relaxation, exercise, meditation, and visualization are all used. The patient learns to visualize the cancer being attacked by his white blood cells and the tumor overwhelmed and becoming smaller, and perhaps to the point of disappearing.

Biofeedback

Biofeedback is a therapeutic procedure designed to put an individual in touch with bodily functions previously thought to be beyond conscious control. These functions include low-level muscle tensions, skin temperatures, blood circulation, brain waves, and heart beat. Becoming consciously aware of these involuntary processes is accomplished by using a biofeedback machine similar in appearance to a small radio. Attached to it are electrodes which are placed on the forehead of the patient to monitor his brain waves. These waves are either amplified and displayed on a dial or are produced as sounds. The brain continuously sends out electrical energy in varying frequencies determined by the nature of its activity. When the body is tensed and is feeling stress, the waves are high intensity beta waves. As the body becomes quiet and relaxed, the waves change to alpha frequencies. Thus, the feedback from the machine helps the patient to experience precisely the feeling state that must be achieved in order to be relaxed. This state can eventually be reached without the machine. Isn't it the American style to use electronics to read ourselves!

Biofeedback, as a therapy, is found to be most effective in treating illnesses that are emotionally based. The Menniger Foundation Clinic in Topeka, Kansas, where the therapy is scientifically controlled, reports good results with many patients.

Acupuncture

Acupuncture is a therapeutic technique based on scientific procedures developed by mystics and seers in ancient India and China. Thousands of years ago these wise men taught that in the healthy body there is a continuous circulation of energy or life force, and when this is blocked by tensions or stress, illness results. When the energy is redirected back to its normal circulation, the individual returns to health. According to these ancient healers, there are seven main energy centers or chakras in the body. Leading into these are over 481 lesser centers and many more invisible meridians which line the limbs, the trunk, and the head of the body. Along these are very sensitive pressure points which relate directly to the different organs and parts of the body. By inserting needles into a number of carefully selected pressure points, the acupuncturist is able to help start the normal circulation of energy to the affected part of the body.

Until only recently very few states have recognized acupuncture as a valid treatment procedure and licensed physicians for its practice. Other states will, no doubt, do so soon in view of the increasing evidence that it is an effective means to alleviate the discomfort of many conditions.

Acupressure

Acupressure and massage are therapies closely related in theory to acupuncture. In this practice the energy is directed through the hands of the healer and transferred to a specific area of the patient's body. Through massage and touching in caring ways an exchange of energy takes place that accelerates the healing process. Studies have shown that this is due to a rise in the hemoglobin, that part of the red blood cells responsible for oxygen uptake from the lungs and its distribution to all the cells in the body. This exchange of energy has been described by individuals who have been treated by acupressure as heat that seems to enter and revitalize the body.

Exercise

As physiologists study the changes that occur in the aging body, they find that the physical deterioration evidenced is very often directly related to a lack of physical activity. So many of us, as we grow older, become careless and let our bodies get out of shape. Abdominal muscles become flabby, and as a result our backs ache. We are afraid to push ourselves too hard, so we become physically lazy. Because some arthritic joints give us pain, we grow daily more adverse to take regular exercise. The human body is built to be active, and some regular exercise is essential to keep it functioning at its peak capacity. Activity not only helps the body maintain its muscle tone, but, more importantly, it accelerates the breathing process and increases the amount of oxygen available through the blood to nourish all of the issues and organ systems. A specific time for daily exercise also provides an opportunity to consciously experience the wonder and rhythms of our bodies and be grateful for how well they have functioned through all the years. As we explore the body movements, we can meditate on the source of the energy of life, opening ourselves to its flow.

With normal aging, vigor may diminish slightly, but most of us, if good health is maintained, can experience reasonable physical energy all through life. Even those of us who have taken little exercise during our adult years can benefit from a program of physical activity introduced during the later years. Doctor Herbert A. deVries, an exercise physiologist at the University of Southern California, recently studied a group of sedentary older men and women. The group participated in a program of increased physical activity under careful controls and supervision. It was found that increased physical activity could be introduced safely and effectively with positive benefits to the health and well-being of these formerly sedentary individuals. The subjects' ability to breathe deeply and efficiently was improved, heart muscles were strengthened, blood pressure was lowered, and the precentage of body fat was reduced.

Any strenuous activity program should be undertaken only after consultation with one's physician. It should of course begin at your present level of fitness and be tailored to your specific physical needs. Not many of us will be found among the joggers, long distance runners, or mountain climbers, but there are few other physical activities that are inappropriate just because our bodies have grown older. For a wide scope of activities you should chose those you most enjoy that are adaptable to your strength and ability.

It is an exhilarating experience to put a favorite record on the stereo and move or dance to the rhythm. If you are feeling bored or depressed you soon find yourself in a different mood. Some of us enjoy walking, hiking, and folk dancing; some prefer golf, bowling, or swimming. For others, geriatric calisthenics or the more esoteric practice of yoga or Tai-Chi-Chuan puts us in touch with our bodies and limbers the joints. Many of these exercises can be done while seated and are, therefore, especially adaptable when your body has become stiff and your balance unsure. They can be performed within the limits of many cardiovascular conditions and when physical responses have slowed down. All of us can, on awakening and while still in bed, stretch heels, then toes, arms over head, stretch one side, then the other, then relax. What exhilaration you can feel from these simple stretches!

Yoga

Yoga as practiced by ancient East Indian and Chinese mystics and modern devotees enables one to control the rational mind and thus achieve an altered state of consciousness. There are many different schools of yoga practice, but Hatha yoga has been the one most popularized in America as an exercise technique. It concentrates on deep breathing to stabilize the rhythm of the breath and bring about complete relaxation of the body. Through a series of stretching positions called asanas, which are held as long as the individual is comfortable and without strain, the body and mind are brought into harmony. A daily practice of yoga not only helps to keep the body muscles in tone but gives one a sense of integration, rejuvenation, and increased self-awareness.

Tai-Chi-Chuan

Tai-Chi-Chuan is an exercise routine based on an old Chinese form of meditation for the martial arts. Its coordinated eye and hand movements are very slow and gentle, starting and ending with deep breathing. The movements are designed to relax the muscles, move all of the joints, and give balance to the total body.

Classes in Hatha yoga and Tai-Chi-Chuan are now offered in the weekly programs of many churches, local YWCAs and YMCAs, senior centers, adult schools, and residences for older people. They offer not only an exercise experience that one can enjoy without your age being a barrier, but they also provide a group experience where you can meet and enjoy younger people as well as your age-mates.

Nutrition

In our health-conscious society diet and nutrition are of interest to young and old alike. There are diets to lose weight, gain weight, lower cholesterol, and to control arthritis, diabetes, allergies, hypoglycemia, and diverticulitis. Diets to control any serious weight problem or physical condition should, of course, be carefully tailored to one's individual needs. A diet should be undertaken only after consultation with a nutritionist or a doctor whose medical training included nutrition.

There are many reasons why some of us develop poor eating habits and, unknowingly, deprive our bodies of elements needed to maintain a delicate chemical balance. The ways in which our food is grown, prepared, and packaged are so different from the days when we were raising our families. How confusing and exhausting it is to shop in supermarkets with their long aisles and endless shelves displaying a bewildering variety of items, when low incomes and the inflationary costs of food restrict the quality and quantity of foods we can afford.

When living alone, shopping for and preparing well-balanced meals becomes, for many of us, a chore and a bore. It is so easy to use frozen and pre-cooked foods, rather than to take the time and effort to prepare fresh fruits and vegetables and a nutritious entree. Often a person eats too much and the wrong kinds of food when lonely and anxious. At these times we try to be "good to ourselves" and soon find that we have added many unwanted pounds. Furthermore, some of us may not be able to get to stores, especially when we have physical infirmities.

Doctor Jean Mayer, Professor of Nutrition at Harvard University, reports that studies of the eating habits of older people have shown that proper nutrition alleviates and can even prevent certain diseases of old age and reverse confusional states which can be due to malnutrition and anemia. Because we are less active than in our youth, we need fewer calories. There appears, at present, no evidence that older people require different nutrition than other mature adults. Most nutritionists recommend that we should avoid gaining weight, should eat a diet high in protein and fiber content, and avoid excessive animal fats and cholesterol. An intake of 2300 calories a day for a man and 2000 for a woman at age seventy and older is recommended.

To keep our bodies well nourished and to enable them to repair themselves, we need, according to Doctor Mayer, a daily diet that includes the following foods: meat, fish, poultry, nuts, beans, milk, cheese, yogurt, and other dairy products; whole grains in cereals and bread; and fresh vegetables and fruits. Such a diet should provide all the essential vitamins and minerals we need. We read with growing concern, however, reports from the Food and Drug Administration that many of these essential elements are removed from certain food items by modern production and processing methods. Chemicals and dyes added as preservatives, coloring, and flavoring agents have been found to be injurious to the human body. We need to study the labels on the contents of the food we buy to avoid taking harmful additives.

The need to supplement our diets with vitamins and minerals is a controversial subject among health professionals. Some think it an expensive way of providing essentials that we should get from our daily food. While vitamins are essential for good health, taking excessive amounts of some can be harmful. The Food and Drug Administration has recently published a pamphlet entitled *A Primer on Vitamins* which lists the food, vitamins, and minerals that we need in our daily diets. It is written in simple language and may be secured without charge from any local Food and Drug office.

The importance of good nutrition to the health of older persons is substantiated by legislation passed by Congress in 1972. The Nutritional Act for Senior Citizens provides that hot meals five days a week be available to all persons over sixty years of age. Through Title VII of the Older Americans Act, funds are granted to the state agencies on aging which, in turn, makes funds available to local communities to establish easily accessible dining sites. There is no charge for the meal, though each participant is expected to contribute what he can. Health education and recreational activities are also a part of these meal programs.

Drugs

I can still hear so clearly the incredulity and disappointment in her voice when my friend Edith called me after a visit to her doctor. She had a heavy cold that had hung on for weeks. Feeling low in energy and all "washed up," she decided to consult her doctor and ask him to prescribe something to "pep her up." "Imagine! All he did," she said, "was to tell me to get plenty of rest, eat a well-balanced diet, and walk at least a mile every day. He said I didn't need any medication, and he wouldn't even prescribe vitamins!"

Without a prescription from a doctor many of us feel that we are being neglected and that our complaints are not receiving serious attention. We expect doctors to work instant cures, and we too readily turn over to them, through the shots they give or the drugs they prescribe, all responsibility to restore us to health. In the early part of this century there were no miracle drugs. A doctor had to depend on his own bedside manner and create confidence and hope by becoming personally involved with his patient. Through this caring relationship the creative energy of the patient could then become operative. Doctor James Fries, an immunologist at Stanford University Medical Center, in his recent book *Take Care of Yourself: A Consumer's Guide to Medical Care,* says that too many of us fail to trust the natural healing processes of our bodies. We depend too heavily on drugs.

We are learning, however, that drugs are not all good! Along with their very real potential to work wonders, there has grown, with their widespread use, the possibility to work real harm. Since 90 percent of the drugs used today were unknown ten years ago, many are still in their experimental stage. Their total effect on the body's tissues and the side effects are still not fully known. A drug may be most effective in treating a specific physical or mental illness while reacting adversely on other parts of the body.

According to a recent Senate hearing on the use of drugs, it was reported that over 100,000 Americans die needlessly every year due to side effects from their misuse and from the treatment-resistant bacteria which have emerged because of the use of antibiotics. If a drug has side effects, and many of them do, the doctor must decide if the benefits outweigh the potential risks involved in its use and discuss this decision with the patient.

The use, misuse, and overuse of drugs by all age groups gives great credence to the fact that we, as Americans, have become an "overmedicated" society. The use of mind-altering drugs and the related increase of violence have become a disturbing part of our youth culture. The dependence of middle-aged men and women on barbiturates, tranquilizers, and alcohol to cope with the pressures and tensions of their everyday lives increases in alarming proportions. The *Washington Post,* in a article entitled "Drug Firms Back Big Promotion," on March 13, 1974, reported that the amount spent on drugs and alcohol in America amounts to $455 million annually.

Drug abuse has also become for us older adults a major problem as our doctors prescribe sedatives and mood-control drugs to numb the physical and psychic suffering that many people experience in their older adult years. Overworked doctors and nurses and medical personnel in geriatric wings of hospitals and nursing homes too often grow impatient with older patients. They readily administer pills to numb the anxieties rather than take the time to support, reassure, and be competently compassionate by helping their patients understand what is happening to them. There is a vast difference between this way of administering drugs to control patients and their positive curative use.

As drugs proliferate, costs increase, and deaths due to misuse mount, the public is demanding stricter controls and legislation to regulate the pharmaceutical companies in the promotion of their products to physicians. Many of us have not known that drugs have generic names as well as brand names, which are designations given them by their manufacturers. Brand names generally cost twice as much as their generic counterparts of the same quality. Many of our states now have laws which allow pharmacists to substitute generic drugs for the more expensive brand name drug. You can reduce drug costs materially by asking your doctor to prescribe drugs by their generic names. The difference in cost between the generic or brand name often differs by as much as 400 percent. You have every right to ask the price of a prescription and to compare prices before handing it over to be filled. Furthermore, it is wise to read the instructions when you pick up a prescription so you can query the druggist about the purpose of the medication, if the doctor's instructions are not clear.

Sometimes a person might recommend a drug that he is taking to a friend who seems to have symptoms similar to his own. This is an unwise practice, since the same drug can have different effects on different people. Also, a drug prescribed for one person may seriously interfere with other drugs the friend may be taking. Another real danger is mixing alcohol and tranquilizers or sleeping pills. This can even be fatal. Drugs frequently are a blessing, but they can also be a curse!

Concluding Reflections

An eighty-five-year-old friend of mine spoke for most of us when he said, "If I had known I was going to live so long, I would have taken better care of myself." It is never too late to start doing this! We can begin by rejecting the myth that illness is an inevitable part of growing old and by remembering that old age itself does not destroy the creative powers of the body and the mind. Our responsibility is to practice self-care by adopting healthful habits of nutrition, exercise, and rest and getting medical care promptly when serious symptoms occur. This plan will take discipline and a tranquil mind to understand and accept the normal changes that take place. We need to listen and hear what our bodies tell us and have patience with our physical frailties. Above all, we need to assume as much responsibility as we are able for our own health and well-being, rather than turning the job totally over to someone else.

Chapter 9

DEALING CREATIVELY WITH DEATH AS A REALITY IN LIFE

> I died as a mineral and became a plant,
> I died as a plant and become an animal,
> I died as an animal and was a man.
> What should I fear?
> When was I less by dying?
>
> OLD EAST INDIAN POEM

WHY a chapter on death and dying in a book on living and growing, you may ask? Death is not extraneous to life; it is an integral part of it. Nor is it new to us who are older. We have experienced death many times, both "little" and "large" ones. At each life stage we have known "little deaths" and "rebirths" of our former selves in new roles and responsibilities. Over the years we have experienced "large deaths" as we have lost those whose lives have validated ours and given them meaning. In times of big "deaths," grief seemed to inundate us until the void was filled, and then we took up living again. Dying, then, is something that we have done many times already, and each death, large and small, has contributed to our growth and continuous renewal.

In this chapter we will not discuss our psychological deaths or the loss of loved persons, but face as realistically as we can the end of our own physical lives.

The Nature of Death Cannot Be Rationally Known

The nature and meaning of death is beyond our rational knowing, for we are finite, and our minds are limited. Death is an experience on another level of consciousness not perceived by our five senses. Chekhov, a nineteenth century Russian author, asked, "And what does it mean, dying?" He then replied, "Perhaps man has a hundred senses and only the five we know are lost to death, while the other ninety-five remain alive." Is it from these other modes of knowing that man's intuitions and longings for immortality have come? Adelaide Love, the poet, also asks the questions in these lines:

> For every need of body or of soul
> That man may feel upon this fevered earth,
> God has devised an answer — knowing all
> His varied cravings from the hour of birth.
> Shall we believe that he allows just one
> Great hunger, deepening through the years to be
> Without its answer — strangely choosing this —
> Man's loftiest cry for immortality?

Whether the idea of personal life continuing beyond death is an illusion or premonition of truth, we do not know. For some people, any discussion of its possibility is just one more example of man's wishful thinking and superstition. For others, immortality through the ages has been a belief based on deep personal religious faith. To put all of our confidence in the measurable, and reject that which lies beyond rational statement, will be to seriously short-change ourselves.

Until recently there has been little objective evidence that life continues after death. Current findings, of an increasing number of highly respected and scientifically based studies of psychic phenomena not explainable by natural laws, cannot be lightly dismissed. Doctor Raymond Moody, in his recent book, *Life after Life,* recounts the out-of-body experiences of a number of patients who had died clinically, which indicate to him that something exists beyond our visible world that transcends death. When successfully resuscitated, these individuals all told of being aware of leaving their bodies while continuing to be conscious of themselves within their human consciousness. Doctor Elisabeth Kübler-Ross, a physician, psychiatrist, and pioneer in helping the terminally ill and their families face death without fear, has written, "Before I started working with the dying, I did not believe in life after death. Now I believe in one, beyond the shadow of a doubt."

The Psychologists Look at Death

As psychologists have studied the final stages of life, they have found that, as physical energies slow down, the self gradually turns from the outer world and attachments to material things, to that of the inner world and a heightening of interest in personal meanings. Commitments to activities, i.e. *doing* which have dominated our lives, give way to more subjective and profound interests of *being*. We now become aware of a consciousness that lies outside of activities which, when we were young were too busy to experience. Psychoanalyst Carl Jung has called this gradual change the "achievement of death." This process of withdrawal from emotional and social involvements becomes accelerated as physical frailty increases, and one is alone with few, if any, survivors. Finally, when one is very old, and energy is at low ebb, the spirit seems to decide that it no longer wants to be housed in a suffering human body. One seems to move into a serene transcendent state of consciousness, a state never experienced before. May Sarton, in her novel, *Plant Dreaming Deep,* describes the death of her mother: "My Mother, through long months of gradual waning, never once complained or begged to be released from pain; she seemed to fold herself inward like a closing flower, to detach herself gently from all she had loved, to 'let go' until she seemed to us to have become nothing but light, an impersonal light, as if there were nothing left for death to take but the soul itself."* It would appear then that when our energies have slowed down and the soul is ready to leave the body, one's readiness for death will seem like the most obvious thing in the world.

Psychological studies of man's conscious and unconscious self point out that man alone, among all living things, is able to stand apart psychologically from himself and observe himself existing in time and space. No experience that one goes through ever seems to involve the whole person. That part of us which is the self, that transcends the ego, always stands apart

*From *Plant Dreaming Deep* by May Sarton. W. W. Norton & Company, Inc., New York, N. Y. Copyright ©1968 by May Sarton.

from and observes the ego as it struggles in time and space, achieves, fails, and contemplates its own nonbeing. This self, according to metaphysical teachers, is the *other within* and is related to and a fragment of the *universal* or *cosmic self*. As the body dies this fragment is thought then to return to and become a part of the Whole, much as the waves become again a part of the ocean as they break on the shore. Man then is not bound and defined totally by the existence of his physical body. There is the larger consciousness of which his individual consciousness is a part. Death is the end of the physical manifestation, but not the end of consciousness. When the physical body dies, the consciousness of the individual is merged with the consciousness of the Whole or God.

Our Fears About Death

We cannot know whether we fear death until we come face to face with our own. Our fear of death is repressed and operates only in our unconscious as a catastrophic force that we can do nothing about. Most of our lives, by a process of denial, we have protected ourselves from anxiety around death. We have fantasized that it happens to others, but not to us.

For most of us the real fears are around the process of dying rather than death itself. Our overriding fears are the possible loss of mastery over our physical functioning, becoming unable to care for ourselves, and the resulting insults and indignities to our bodies and spirits. We fear pain and our ability to handle it and the loneliness of dying when no one is near to comfort us. Then there is the nagging fear that our savings may not be adequate to meet the cost of our care and that we may become a burden on our families, draining them of emotional and financial resources. These are the real fears with which we find it so hard to cope.

Our Meanings Around Death Are Related to Our Meanings About Life

Death as an integral part of human existence is as natural

and predictable as being born. Each of us must formulate his own philosophy and faith by which he is able to face and accept it. Our ability to integrate this new experience that awaits us into our conscious thinking will depend on the quality of our total orientation to life and its meaning. Since traditional theology too often lags far behind the sophisticated findings in other fields in its understanding of the nature of man and the cosmos, it is often unable to communicate its teachings to modern man. We find ourselves, therefore, sometimes bereft of a system of dependable meanings with which to respond to death.

All religious faiths and denominations have their distinctive and well-developed theologies and beliefs about life after death, and each has important meanings and values to its adherents. However, a religious faith that is based on an unquestioning acceptance of traditional theological beliefs, which the mind of modern man no longer finds intellectually honest and tenable, may not prove adequate to meet our fears and despair as we face death. If, on the other hand, our faith and meanings around death have kept pace with the findings of the scientists who have split the atom and the space age that has plunged us into a new understanding of the universe and expanded our minds into new dimensions, then we may be better able to contemplate and accept death. It will be, for us, not an experience that terminates life but a changing of consciousness of being one with all Being, which is changeless — creating, dissolving, and recreating. We will believe, along with the poet William Blake, that, "If the doors of perception were cleansed everything would appear to us as it is — Infinite."

The Time of Death is Controlled Today by Medical Technology

How many times on losing a loved one have we said, "The Lord giveth and the Lord taketh away. Blessed be the name of the Lord." Death has been thought of as "the will of God" or an "act of fate." Today, the time of death has moved into the realm of human control as medical technology makes it possible to sustain life by artificial supports of the body's circulation, respiration, and nutrition systems. Through these life-prolonging techniques, the medical profession is now able to delay the act of dying.

The fact that the moment of death, when the brain has ceased to function, can now be delayed for days, weeks, and even months by highly artificial and costly means raises many moral and legal questions. Our moral heritage does not yet accept intentional death; current laws in most states restrict the freedom to die and threaten the physician and family with murder if life supports are withheld. Ethical, religious, and legal issues are involved around who is to make the decision to allow someone to die. Pope Paul XII stated that when a person is in a coma and beyond recovery there is no need to employ "extraordinary means" to keep him alive. According to Jewish law, when a person suffers irreversible brain damage and can no longer recite a "bracha," a blessing to praise God, or perform a "mitzvah," an act to help his fellowman, there is nothing to save. It is then an act of compassion to no longer artificially prolong breathing and heart beat since death is inevitable. Among Protestant denominations there is no specific position; the viewpoints vary according to the fundamental or liberal theology of the denomination. Throughout the western world there is evidence of increasing urgency to rethink the definitions of death and the rights of each individual to make the decision of when he chooses to die.

Right-To-Die Laws Being Enacted in Some States

California, Idaho, Arkansas, New Mexico, and Oregon are the only states that have enacted natural death laws. Proposed legislation has been defeated in some forty other states. All the laws are based on a "living will" document that authorizes physicians to withhold extraordinary methods in hopeless cases. The California law does not give anyone permission to end the life of another in a mercy-killing manner. The document is a simple statement that one does not want his or her life prolonged artificially after the physician decides that there is no hope for recovery. A doctor must honor a patient's request if *all* of the following conditions are met:

- The patient has been examined and diagnosed as being terminally ill by two doctors.
- Fourteen days or more *after* such diagnosis, the patient signs a formal Directive to Physicians, the wording of which is prescribed by law. (No other so-called Living Wills are acceptable under the law.)
- The Directive to Physicians is witnessed by two people, neither of whom is related by blood or marriage to the patient, nor entitled to any part of the patient's estate by probate law or terms of the patient's will, nor doctors or persons employed by the health care facility involved.
- The law also provides that people who are not terminally ill can execute a Directive to Physicians at any time as an expression of their desires, should they become terminally ill. Doctors are not required to honor the directive, however, unless it is re-executed by the patient fourteen or more days after the diagnosis of a terminal illness. Should one desire to execute a directive, it should be kept by a member of one's immediate family or attorney.

Some of my friends who live in states that have no laws and who wish to participate in the decision about when they will die if there is no hope for recovery have signed, while they are still well, a Living Will. This is a simple statement that should be signed in the presence of witnesses and given to a family member, one's doctor, attorney, and clergyman. It can, of course, be revoked at any time. Although there is still question in many states concerning its legality, it does give those closest to us an indication of our wishes. It states,

TO MY FAMILY, MY PHYSICIAN,
MY CLERGYMAN, MY LAWYER*

If the time comes when I can no longer take part in decisions for my future, let this statement stand as the testament of my

*This form is available from the Euthanasia Council, 250 W. 57th Street, New York, 10019.

wishes:

If there is no reasonable expectation of my recovery from physical or mental disability, I ________________ request that I be allowed to die and not be kept alive by artificial means or heroic measures. Death is as much a reality as birth, growth, maturity and old age; it is the one certainty. I do not fear death as much as I fear the indignity of deterioration, dependence and hopeless pain. I ask that drugs be mercifully administered to me for terminal suffering even if they hasten the moment of death.

This request is made after careful consideration. Although this document is not legally binding, you who care for me will, I hope, feel morally bound to follow its mandate. I recognize that it places a heavy burden of responsibility upon you, and it is with the intention of sharing that responsibility and mitigating any feelings of guilt that this statement is made.

Signed ________________

Date ______________

Witnessed by:

____

____

Choosing the Time of Death

Death occurs, of course, not only by accident and as a result of illness but also by intent. Many people feel that the option of deciding when they will die, if there is no hope of recovery, is a basic human right and the ultimate affirmation of human freedom. "I shall put my house in order," they say, "and then end my life at what seems to me to be the right time for the release of my spirit." They are comfortable with the thought of dying and have made no hasty decision. Other people interpret the taking of one's own life to avoid suffering as a wrongful act. Doctor Sidney L. Pressey, Professor Emeritus of Psychology at Ohio State University, writing in the *Gerontologist* for August, 1977, asks a basic question:

> At the age of 88, crippled by rheumatism, plagued by insomnia, of failing vision, must I wait out a natural death, perhaps by becoming mindless, incontinent, locked in the

back ward of a nursing "home"? Do I have any rights as to the nature of my dying? I suggest that those of us who are now old and ill and dying have a special responsibility to speak out about such matters, and seek to shape public opinion and the law into accord with such realities.

New Ways of Caring for the Dying

In our childhood, people usually died in their homes with their families around them. Today, caring for the ill and dying is becoming increasingly the responsibility of institutions other than the family. At least 90 percent of us, it is estimated, will die in hospitals or nursing homes. Acute hospitals, for most of us, are strange and awesome places where staff members have been trained primarily in technical skills to care and rehabilitate patients. The dying patient, who needs warmth and compassion as well as good technical care, feels terrifyingly isolated and lonely. This is particularly true of patients without families and only a few friends. Many doctors and young nurses are not personally comfortable around the dying and are reluctant to spend time with them. Changes are coming, however. Although up-to-date geriatric nursing care is not yet found in all hospitals, it is a new subspeciality in nursing education. Here the emphasis is on caring *about* as well as caring *for* patients and serving along with chaplains in counselling the dying and their families.

If death has not occurred in the hospital before Medicare benefits were exhausted, family members then face the alternative of caring for their relative in one of their homes or in a nursing home. In our society the nursing home has, in fact, become the place where older people, especially those without families to care for them, must go to die. The nursing home industry has grown by leaps during the past three decades. Many are sponsored by church and nonprofit groups, but the greater number are extensions of hospitals or are units of large proprietary corporations. In order to maintain high standards of safety and nursing care, these institutions are licensed and inspected by state health departments. Many nursing homes give excellent care to their patients; others make the last days of the elderly patient a veritable nightmare. Because of the necessity to improve the quality of care in nursing homes generally, the National Citizen's Coalition for Nursing Homes has been formed to develop national strategies and standards for their operation. This coalition, along with other consumer action groups and proposed legislation, will hopefully result in high standards of care for patients.

The Hospice Movement

A new and more humane way of caring for dying patients is being developed in some communities. It challenges the system that says the only way to die is in a nursing home or under intensive care in a hospital. It is called Hospice. The emphasis of care of terminally ill patients is on compassionate pain control, the elimination of loneliness, preservation of personal dignity, and the conservation of the patient's energy. The patient is cared for by a team composed of a physician, nurse, social worker, and clergyman in the patient's own home where he remains for as long as possible. If necessary, the patient can move back and forth from home to hospital or nursing home as conditions demand.

The name hospice comes from the Middle Ages when religious groups provided way-stations for crusaders to and from the Holy Land. Words like hospitality and hospital grew from the same root word as hospice. The first hospice, St. Christopher's, was established by Doctor Cicely Saunders in London in 1949. There are presently only two licensed ones in this country but approximately fifty more are in the planning stage in the United States, and one in Canada. The first was founded in New Haven, Connecticut, in 1974 and the second in Marin County, California, in 1975; the hospice in Canada is in Montreal. Hopefully, the growing interest in death with dignity will lead to the establishment of hospices in all communities. Some hospice programs serve only cancer patients; others are able to minister to dying persons regardless of the illness causing the terminal condition.

The hospice program emphasizes helping the patient live as fully and normally as possible in the time he has left. Patients are encouraged to make their own decisions about their care and retain as much control as possible over their own lives. Although hospice workers go into hospitals and nursing homes when the patient is being cared for there, the intent of the program is to care for the patient in his own home, if he has one. There, in familiar and comfortable surroundings, a patient lives as normally as possible, and family members are encouraged and trained to share in the patient's care with the medical team. The management of pain is the heart of the treatment program so as to enable the patient to maintain alertness and emotional composure and make the best use of his last days. A drug preparation called Hospice Mix is given on a continuing basis for pain control. The patient is closely monitored and the dosage adjusted to the point where the patient is free from pain. He does not become drugged and drowsy but remains alert and functioning. Through pain relief, good home nursing, and the involvement of the family physician and clergy, a patient dies a comfortable, dignified, and natural death, without being attached to machines and tubes to artificially prolong his life.

Once the patient is comfortable, the hospice staff turns its attention to family problems, enabling the family to talk out their fears, regrets, disappointments, and grief. Many times families are so intent on maintaining a brave front for the dying that they are unable to express their feelings unless encouraged by a skilled helper. Hospice workers contact appropriate service agencies to help the family in appropriate ways. Volunteers with legal advice may help the patient in making a will and winding up unfinished business. The hospice team does not feel their responsibility ends when the patient dies, but continues their contacts with the family for as long as necessary to help them through their grief and bereavement. Doctor William Lamers, the founder of the Marin County, California, hospice, says that there is a limit to what hospices can do to cure, but no limit to what they can do to care.

Getting Our Affairs in Order

We have lived too long to be easily deceived either by ourselves or others. Yet, when we are faced with terminal illness, we may continue the denial and waver between wanting to know and not wanting to. A doctor who is honest and really concerned will consider the ability of his patient to handle the diagnosis and when and who should reveal the seriousness of the illness. We may then have an opportunity to do and say the things that will round out our lives in meaningful and healing ways. There will be time to take care of legal and other important business matters, to say goodbye, and to admit our fears as well as share our deepest feelings of faith and love with those who come to sit by the bed and hold our hands. Then, hopefully, quiet moments of accepting what we know to be the inevitable will follow.

If we have managed our lives responsibly and well during earlier periods, we will want, while we are still able, to get our personal affairs in order. This will include making plans and informing our families or friends of our wishes when we die for the disposition of our bodies and the celebration of our lives. These will not be easy steps to take, but we will feel a sense of deep relief and pride when our plans have been completed.

In addition to a will, which should be properly drawn up by a lawyer, it will be helpful to keep some factual data in a personal record book to provide a guide for one's survivors for attending to the funeral, obituary, and other matters. Forms for setting down all pertinent information for the death certificate, funeral arrangements, and other related matters are available from several sources, one of which is the Continental Association of Funeral and Memorial Societies, Inc., at 1828 L Street, N.W., Washington, D. C.

Options We Can Make About What Happens After Death

There are options today concerning what we want to happen to our bodies after death and by what rites we prefer to have our lives celebrated. To ease the immediate problems that will face those we leave behind, we need to think about these options and let our desires be known. Because of high costs, questionable meaning, and psychological support to those who survive, traditional funerals with a public service and expensive casket are being critically evaluated by many today. Studies show that some funeral directors often exploit the grief of the survivors by encouraging them to choose expensive caskets and elaborate funeral services as an expression of their love and respect for the deceased; however, ostentation is hardly a realistic criteria to measure love. Although death benefits from insurances and lump sum final Social Security payments of $255 help meet the cost, funeral expenses still, in many instances, impose financial hardships on survivors. A recent survey made of major metropolitan areas disclose that the average funeral and burial costs are $1500 or more.

An increasing number of people today are choosing cremation as a clean, orderly process for returning human remains to the elements. With the rising cost of land for burials and, in some areas, the shortage of land, cremation is becoming more popular, and crematories are steadily increasing in number. Their charges for services range from $75 to $150. In some cities religious groups or private citizens may obtain the necessary death certificate and permits for transporation and cremation. In other places a funeral director is required. Ashes may be stored indefinitely or mailed by parcel post for burial in another city. Some families prefer to scatter ashes in a favorite garden or woods, into the sea, or from a moutain top, but a few states have laws prohibiting this. Most religions sanction cremation. A Roman Catholic may now request permission from the bishop of his diocese, and requests are usually granted. However, the Greek and Jewish Orthodox faiths and some other religious groups still oppose cremation.

While a traditional funeral arranged by the survivors with a local mortuary is still common practice, there is an alternative choice, i.e. joining a memorial or funeral society, organizations which today are found in over 100 cities across the country. These are nonprofit societies organized by church, labor, civic, and educational groups. Their purpose is to provide simple, dignified, and economical arrangements for after-death services. Services arranged through such a society costs from $150 to $400. A person may join one of these societies for a life-time membership fee of from $10 to $20. After joining, the new member is provided with a listing of the cooperating funeral directors in one's area. It then must be decided what kind of funeral is preferred and at what cost. A copy of the form bearing this information goes to the funeral director designated, and another copy should be kept in one's personal record book. When death occurs, a survivor calls the funeral society, and the services that have been stipulated are provided. Since all funeral societies in this country maintain reciprocal relationships, there is no worry if one should move to a different area.

Whether the funeral is directed by a mortuary or a funeral society, we again have alternative choices between a traditional funeral service or a memorial service. In the former, the casket is present, and the body is often viewed by the mourners. In a memorial service, the remains are not present. The personality of the person and the celebration of his life is central. For a growing number of people a memorial service provides the most appropriate and healing way to work through personal feelings of loss, guilt, and grief.

Still other people, motivated by the desire to make a contribution to medical science and to save the expense of funerals, will their bodies to medical schools for research or specific organs for transplants and tissue banks. Physicians, memorial societies, and funeral directors can help a donor arrange for such gifts. A donor's card such as the following, which is a legal document in most states and provinces, is carried by the donor. Most states also provide donor forms on the backs of drivers' licenses.

UNIFORM DONOR CARD

Of ____

(print or type)

in the hope that I may help others, I hereby make this anatomical gift, if medically acceptable, to take effect upon my death. The words and marks below indicate my desires.

I give: (a) __________ any needed organs or parts

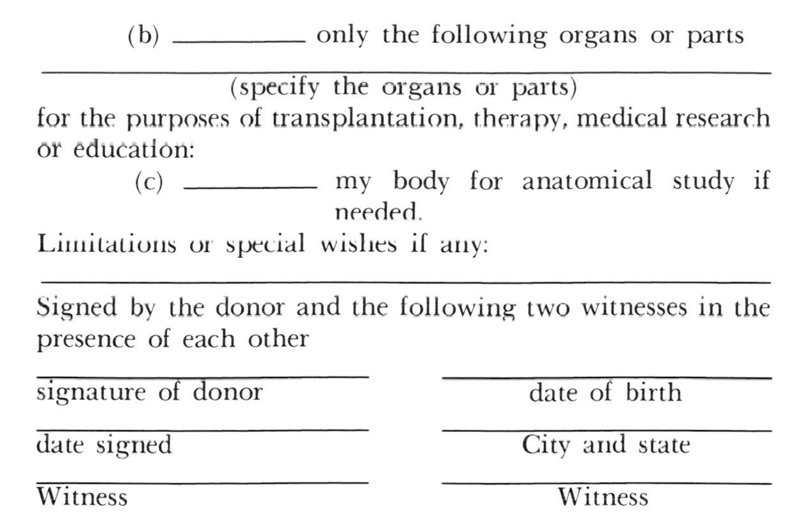

(b) __________ only the following organs or parts

____

(specify the organs or parts)

for the purposes of transplantation, therapy, medical research or education:

(c) __________ my body for anatomical study if needed.

Limitations or special wishes if any:

____

Signed by the donor and the following two witnesses in the presence of each other

______________________	______________________
signature of donor	date of birth
date signed	City and state
Witness	Witness

Concluding Thoughts on Death

Facing one's death, getting personal and financial affairs in order, and making decisions about the funeral triggers in most of us deep emotional stress and anxiety. To handle feelings around the reality of nonbeing is a difficult psychological task, yet it is only the awareness of death limiting life that forces us to see our lives as a totality. Being born, growing, maturing, declining, and dying are according to the laws of all nature. In this we have no option. We can only say yes to life in its entirety. To be able to do so is the ultimate goal of growth. It makes the difference in the quality of our remaining days.

Such a total philosophy was so beautifully demonstrated to me in the life of Mrs. Y. Over a period of several months I had been driving Mrs. Y., a widow without children who lives at Springwood, a retirement residence, to her internist for a series of appointments and tests. As she came from his office after her last appointment, she seemed unusually frail and pale and glad for my arm to steady her as we walked to the car. Mrs. Y. was quiet and withdrawn as we drove back to Springwood, and I sensed that here was a silence that I should not, at that time, try to invade. It was lunchtime at Springwood when we returned, but she said that she would prefer to go to her apartment and have some tea and toast. I said goodbye, assured her that I would be in touch with her soon, and then sought out the nurse to report that I felt apprehensive about Mrs. Y. and asked that she visit her soon.

Several days later I noticed some lovely buds on my rose bushes. I thought of Mrs. Y. and decided to take them to her. She seemed so happy to see me and anxious to share with me what she had previously not been able to. With no overtones of self-pity, anxiety, or fear, she told me that her final medical tests showed that she had an inoperable cancer. The news had shaken her. Then, with the help of her minister and her closest friend, she had been able to face the reality of her condition and the challenge of how she would use whatever time remained to her. She said that it was like having a second chance at life. She filled her days with recalling and reliving all of the experiences and travels, pleasures and sorrows, successes and failures that had made her life meaningful. She listened again to the recordings of music she had loved, and took time to write long letters to her grandchildren, affirming her love and faith in them. She promised her friends to help, as long as she was able, to make braille transcriptions for the blind members of her church. There was a light in her eye and lilt in her voice as she told me that she had decided that she would make the best of her precious time, however long that might be. "When you know for sure that your life will soon be over, you learn to give up worrying about little things," she confided as I left her one day. Mrs. Y. had learned that, as the amount of time we have to live is shortened, each day gains in relative value, since it becomes a greater proportion of our remaining days.

How magnificently, too, former Vice-President Humphrey made us aware that the way people face death expresses the quality of their lives as clearly as the way they have lived. His first public appearance, after leaving the hospital where an inoperable cancer was diagnosed, was to address a labor convention. "I'm not about to have someone cover me up," he announced. "I'm not about ready to get lost. I'm about ready to be found again." What a triumphant spirit! In facing death Senator Humphrey so courageously demonstrated that our lives are to be lived as fully as possible to the last days and that our mortality must not only be accepted but transcended. To meet death thus becomes the crowning achievement of a fully lived life.

Chapter 10

DEVELOPING A PHILOSOPHY ABOUT AGING

In the midst of winter
I finally learned
That there was in me
An invincible summer
ALBERT CAMUS*

IN all nature the seasons of the year are marked by an orderly process of planting, flowering, maturing, and harvesting. So, also, the years of our lives are defined by a continuous unfolding of our physical, mental, spiritual, and social selves, through infancy, childhood, adulthood, and old age. As each season of the year has its own distinctive character and peculiar beauty, so each life stage has had its own natural rhythms of maturation, meanings, and satisfactions. Since old age is the time for the body to eventually fail, it has become, for many of us, an unwelcome and threatening season. We deny and reject it and thus fail to integrate its potential values and gifts into our lives.

As members of a society that tends to depreciate old people, we have too long tried to protect our little egos by denying what we know to be true, that we are indeed old. In becoming a part of such a conspiracy of denial, we miss the sense of the preciousness and flow of life and the harvest that awaits our older years.

Today a new wind is blowing. Though ever so slowly, society's attitudes toward aging are changing. The prospect that old age can be a meaningful and creative time of life is becoming each year more of a possibility for more of us. This is

---

*From Albert Camus, "L'ete (Summer)," *Lyrical and Critical Essays,* trans. Ellen Conroy Kennedy, and ed. Philip Thody (New York, Random House, Inc., Alfred A. Knopf, Inc., 1970).

not the time for us to withdraw to the sidelines and conclude that we are no longer needed. We must stay actively involved for as long as we are able and be open to what is happening around us. We must remain vocal and aggressive in our criticism of our society when it tries to shut out and ignore the elderly.

Each of us has made his own life journey and dealt with his own personal facts, both joyous and tragic. There have been times when all of us have been led where we would not have chosen to go — through illness and frailty, separation and loss, loneliness and longing. We have met challenges and difficulties, and many of us have survived against terrible odds. Many times now we are aware that we have too often in the past settled for little bits and pieces of life. We have allowed the tyranny of external circumstances to take over, rather than having had faith in our own capacity for growth. We realize that from the freedom to choose our inner reactions to our outer circumstances has come our integrity and strength. Now we can look back and claim our lives and whatever we have made of them. We know where we have been, what is important, what values we have tested with our lives and found good. We know who needs us, what comes first, and what we can do without. Often out of necessity, but also because we knew that the resources of our planet were limited, we have learned to live more simply, to conserve and recycle rather than waste. Most importantly, we have learned that it is people that matter most, and that life seems to make more sense if lived on a caring human scale rather than on an impersonal mass one. We agree with Jess in Jessamyn West's *Friendly Persuasion,* when he said to his wife, "Eliza, I'm eighty years old. All my life I've been trying to do people good. Whether that was right or not I don't know, but it comes over me now that I'm excused from all that . . . From now on Eliza, I don't figure there is a thing asked of me but to love my fellowmen."*

At times, some of us seem no longer interested in reaching

---

*From Jessamyn West, *Friendly Persuasion* (New York, Harcourt Brace Jovanovich, 1956).

for the future, but often fear it instead. We experience days that are difficult, as well as times when it seems well with us. There are times when we feel depleted. Then we will need to shed responsibilities that we carry and be good to ourselves, acknowledging and accepting that this is the way we are for a time. From such times will eventually come the capacity to bear our anxieties and let them be a stimulus toward some fresh new dimensions of self-discovery and growth.

Doctor Howard Thurman, Emeritus Dean of the Chapel of Boston University, tells this story:

> One day as I visited a farmer in his apple orchard, he picked from the tree two apples and gave them to me. I noticed that each had a deep scar on its skin, and around this scar the apple itself was shriveled, while the rest of it had developed into a beautiful piece of fruit. The farmer explained it this way:
>
> "When the apples were very young a hail storm had bruised them very deeply. These particular apples did not, like some of the others that had been so damaged, fall off of the tree and rot. They did live. It was as if they had decided to absorb as much as possible of the hail storm and go on with the business of living; that is, the business of realizing themselves and becoming the best apples possible under the circumstances."

There is inherent in all of us, as in the apples, a life force that enables each of us to carry on with the business of living and meet our personal problems without giving up.

In old age, then, we have two options. We can give up and allow our lives to gradually diminish into meaningless apathy, or we can move courageously into dimensions of growth that will allow us to achieve new levels of self-realization and tie our own small meanings into cosmic meanings. Which option we choose will depend not on any specific conditions or circumstances of our lives but on our decisions of how we will use our spiritual freedom to meet and handle our daily realities. The measure of our personal meanings and inner security will lie in our ability to say, in the words of Dag Hammarskjold, the first Secretary General of the United Nations,

. . . Night is drawing nigh . . .
For all that has been . . . thanks!
For all that shall be . . . Yes.*

---

*From Dag Hammarskjold, *Markings*, trans. Leif Sjoberg and W. H. Auden (New York, Random House, Alfred A. Knopf, 1964).

BIBLIOGRAPHY

CHAPTER 1

Butler, Robert: *Why Survive Being Old in America.* New York, Harper and Row Publishers, 1975.

Harrington, Michael: *Fragments of the Century.* New York, Saturday Review Press, 1974.

Heilbroner, Robert: *An Inquiry Into the Human Prospect.* New York, W. W. Norton and Company, 1974.

Leonard, George B.: *The Transformation.* New York, Delacorte Press, 1972.

Paull, Irene: *Everybody's Studying Us.* San Francisco, Glide Urban Center Publications, 1976.

Reich, Charles A.: *Greening of America.* New York, Random House, 1970.

Roszak, Theodore: *Where the Wasteland Ends.* New York, Doubleday and Company, 1973.

Schumacher, E. F.: *Small Is Beautiful.* New York, Harper and Row Publishers, 1973.

Toffler, Alvin: *Future Shock.* New York, Random House, 1970.

Townsend, Claire: *Old Age, The Last Segregation: The Report on Nursing Homes.* Ralph Nader Study Group Reports, New York, Grossman Publishers, 1971.

CHAPTER 2

Comfort, Alex: *A Good Age.* New York, Crown Publishers, 1976.

Dyer, Wayne: *Erroneous Zones.* New York, Funk and Wagnalls Company, 1976.

Erikson, Erik H.: *Childhood and Society.* New York, W. W. Norton and Company, 1963.

Huychk, Margaret H.: *Growing Older.* Englewood Cliffs, New Jersey, Prentice-Hall, 1974.

Jung, Carl: *Modern Man In Search of a Soul.* New York, Harcourt Brace Jovanovich, 1955.

Maslow, Abraham: *Toward a Psychology of Being.* Cincinnati, Ohio, Van Nostrand Reinhold Company, 1962.

Stonecypher, D. D.: *Getting Older and Staying Young.* New York, W. W. Norton and Company, 1974.

Thomas, Lewis: *Lives of a Cell: Notes of a Biology Watcher.* New York, Viking Press, 1974.

Tournier, Paul: *Learn to Grow Old.* New York, Harper and Row Publishers, 1973.

CHAPTER 3

Armour, Richard: *Going Like Sixty.* New York, McGraw-Hill Book Company, 1974.

Busse, Edward and Pfeiffer, Eric: *Behavior and Adaption in Late Life.* Boston, Little, Brown & Company, 1977.

Butler, Robert and Lewis, Myrna I.: *Aging and Mental Health.* St. Louis, C. V. Mosby Company, 1973.

Jackins, Harvey: *The Human Side of Human Beings.* Seattle, Rational Island Publishers, 1965.

May, Rollo: *Man's Search for Himself.* New York, W. W. Norton and Company, 1953.

Neugarten, Bernice: *Middle Age and Aging.* Chicago, University of Chicago Press, 1968.

Newman, Mildred and Berkowitz, Bernard: *How to Be Your Own Best Friend.* New York, Random House, 1971.

Rogers, Mary: *Women and Money.* San Francisco, San Francisco Books, in press.

Selye, Hans: *Stress Without Distress.* Philadelphia, J. B. Lippincott Company, 1974.

CHAPTER 4

Alexander, Zane: *Till Death Do Us Part or Something Else Comes Up.* Philadelphia, Westminster Press, 1976.

Burnside, Irene: *Sexuality and Aging.* Los Angeles, University of Southern California Press, 1975.

Butler, Robert and Lewis, Myrna I.: *Sex After Sixty: A Guide for Men and Women for Their Later Years.* New York, Harper and Row Publishers, 1976.

Hochschild, Arlie: *The Unexpected Community.* Englewood Cliffs, New Jersey, Prentice-Hall, 1973.

Howe, Helen: *Fires of Autumn.* Forest Hills, New York, Queens House, 1976.

Lewis, Alfred and Berns, Barrie: *Three Out of Four Wives.* New York, MacMillan Publishing Company, 1975.

Lopata, Helen: *Widowhood In An American City.* Cambridge, Massachusetts, Schenkman Publishing Company, 1973.

Masters, William and Johnson, Virginia: *Human Sexual Response.* Boston, Little, Brown & Company, 1966.

Peterson, James A. and Briley, Michael: *Widows and Widowhood: A Creative Approach to Being Alone.* New York, Association Press, 1977.
Peterson, James A. and Payne, Barbara: *Love In the Later Years.* New York, Association Press, 1975.
Scheingold, Lee D. and Wagner, Nathaniel: *Sound Sex and the Aging Heart.* New York, Human Sciences Press, 1974.

CHAPTER 5

Galton, Lawrence: *Don't Give Up on An Aging Parent.* New York, Crown Publishers, 1975.
Lasky, Kathryn: *I Have Four Names for My Grandfather.* Boston, Little, Brown & Company, 1976.
L'Engle, Madeleine: *The Summer of the Great Grandmother.* New York, Farrar, Straus and Giroux, 1974.
Otten, Jane and Shelly, Florence: *When Your Parents Grow Old.* New York, Funk and Wagnalls Company, 1976.
Silverstone, Barbara and Hyman, Helen: *You and Your Aging Parent.* New York, Pantheon Books, 1976.

CHAPTER 6

Irwin, Theodore: *After 65: Resources for Self-Reliance.* New York, Public Affairs Committee, Pamphlet No. 501, 1973.
Lynch, James J.: *The Broken Heart: The Medical Consequences of Loneliness.* New York, Basic Books, 1977.
Moustakas, Clark E.: *Loneliness.* Englewood Cliffs, New Jersey, Prentice-Hall, 1961.
Slater, Philip: *The Pursuit of Loneliness.* Boston, Beacon Press, 1970.
Tanner, Ira: *Loneliness: The Fear of Love.* New York, Harper and Row Publishers, 1973.
Tournier, Paul: *Escape From Loneliness.* Philadelphia, Westminster Press, 1976.

CHAPTER 7

Arthur, Julietta: *Retire to Action: A Guide to Volunteer Services.* Nashville, Abingdon Press, 1970.
Babic, A.: The older volunteer: expectations and satisfactions. *Gerontologist, 12*:87-90, 1972.
Fisher, Jerome and Pierce, Robert C.: Dimensions of intellectual functioning in the aged. *J Gerontol, 22*:166-173, 1976.
Hessel, Dieter: *Maggie Kuhn on Aging.* Philadelphia, Westminster Press,

1977.

Jeffers, E. and Nichols, C.: The relationship of activities and attitudes to physical well-being in old people. *J Gerontol, 16*:67-70, 1961.

Kleyman, Paul: *Senior Power: Growing Old Rebelliously*. San Francisco, Glide Urban Center Publications, 1974.

Sainer, Janet S. and Zonder, M. L.: *Serve: Older Volunteers in Community Service*. New York, Community Service Society, 1971.

U. S. Administration on Aging: *Designs for Action for Older Americans. A Project Report on Group Volunteer Service*. Washington, D. C. Government Printing Office, G.O.A. Publication No. 905, 1969.

CHAPTER 8

Benson, Herbert: *The Relaxation Response*. New York, William Morrow and Company, 1975.

Brown, Barbara B.: *New Mind, New Body Biofeedback*. New York, Harper and Row Publishers, 1974.

Clark, Linda: *Help Yourself to Health*. New York, Pyramid Publications, 1974.

Cousins, Norman: Anatomy of an illness. *Saturday Review*, May 28, 1977, pp. 00-00.

De Vries, Herbert: *Vigor Regained*. Englewood Cliffs, New Jersey, Prentice-Hall, 1974.

Downing, George: *Massage and Meditation*. New York, Random House/Bookworks, 1974.

Dychtwald, Kenneth; *Bodymind*. New York, Pantheon Books, 1977.

Geba, Bruno: *Vitality Training for Older Adults*. New York, Random House, 1975.

Geba, Bruno: *Breathe Away Your Tensions*. New York, Random House/Bookworks, 1973.

Karlins, Marvin and Andrews, Lewis: *Biofeedback: Turning On the Power of Your Mind*. New York, Warner Books, 1973.

Keleman, Stanley: *Your Body Speaks Its Mind*. New York, Simon and Schuster, 1975.

Le Shan, Lawrence: *How to Meditate*. Boston, Little, Brown & Company, 1974.

Oyle, Irving: *The Healing Mind*. Milbrae, California, Celestial Arts Publishing Company, 1975.

Pelletier, Kenneth: *Mind as Healer, Mind as Slayer*. New York, Harper and Row Publishers, 1976.

Robbins, Jhan and Fisher, David: *Tranquility Without Pills*. Des Plaines, Illinois, Bantam Books, 1975.

Roberts, Jane: *The Nature of Personal Reality*. Englewood Cliffs, New Jersey, Prentice-Hall, 1974.

Rockstein, Morris and Sussman, Marvin: *Nutrition, Longevity, and Aging.* New York, Academic Press, 1977.

Samuels, Mike and Bennet, Hal: *The Well-Body Book.* New York, Random House, 1974.

Sehnert, Keith and Eisenberg, Howard: *How to Be Your Own Doctor (Sometimes).* New York, Grosset and Dunlap, 1975.

Shealy, Norman: *Ninety Days to Self-Health.* New York, Dial Press, 1977.

Silverman, Milton and Lee, Philip R.: *Pills, Profits, and Politics.* Berkeley, University of California Press, 1974.

Taylor, Robert B.: *Feeling Alive After Sixty-Five.* New York, Arlington House Publishers, 1973.

Vickery, Donald and Fries, James F.: *Take Care of Yourself: A Consumer's Guide to Medical Care.* Reading, Massachusetts, Addison-Wesley Publishing Company, 1976.

Williams, Roger J.: *Nutrition Against Disease.* Des Plaines, Illinois, Bantam Books, 1973.

CHAPTER 9

Arvio, Raymon P.: *The Cost of Dying and What You Can Do About It.* New York, Harper and Row Publishers, 1974.

Feifel, H. (Ed.): *The Meaning of Death.* New York, McGraw-Hill Book Company, 1959.

Hendin, D.: *Death As a Fact of Life.* New York, Warner Books, 1974.

Keleman, Stanley: *Living Your Dying.* New York, Random House, 1976.

Knight, Alice: *The Meaning of Teilhard de Chardin.* Old Greenwich, Connecticut, The Devin-Adair Company, 1974.

Koestenbaum, P.: *Is There An Answer to Death?* Englewood Cliffs, New Jersey, Prentice-Hall, 1976.

Kron, J.: Designing a better place to die. *New Yorker,* March 1, 1975, pp. 43-49.

Kübler-Ross, Elisabeth: *On Death and Dying.* New York, Macmillan Publishing Company, 1970.

Kubler-Ross, Elisabeth: *Death: The Final Stage of Growth.* Englewood Cliffs, New Jersey, Prentice-Hall, 1975.

Margolius, Sidney: *Funeral Costs and Death Benefits.* New York, Public Affairs Committee, Pamphlet No. 409, 1967.

McCoy, Marjorie Casebier: *To Die With Style.* Nashville, Abingdon Press, 1974.

Mitford, Jessica: *The American Way of Death.* New York, Simon and Schuster, 1963.

Moody, Raymond Jr.: *Life After Life.* Covington, Georgia, Mockingbird Books, 1975.

Morgan, Ernest: *A Manual of Death Education.* Burnsville, North Carolina,

Celo Press, 1977.
Pattison, E. Mansell: *The Experience of Dying*. Englewood Cliffs, New Jersey, Prentice-Hall, 1977.
Rosenfeld, Stephen: *The Time of Their Dying*. New York, W. W. Norton and Company, 1977.
Russell, O. Ruth: *Freedom to Die*. New York, Human Sciences Press, 1975.
Saunders, Cecely: *Care of the Dying*. London, MacMillan Publishing Company, 1959.

CHAPTER 10

Kenney, Leon F.: *Memories and Meditations*. Philadelphia, Westminster Press, 1976.
McClay, Elsie: *Green Water*. New York, Thomas Y. Crowell Company, 1977.
Nouwen, Henri J. and Gaffney, Walter: *Aging: The Fulfillment of Life*. New York, Doubleday and Company, 1974.
Schuckman, Terry: *Aging Is Not for Sissies*. Philadelphia, Westminster Press, 1975.
Tournier, Paul: *Learn to Grow Old*. New York, Harper and Row Publishers, 1973.

INDEX

T

U

V

W

Y